GEORGENE SUMMERS

101 THINGS
that piss me off
EXPLETIVES FROM BEHIND CLOSED DOORS

WARNING:
NOT POLITICALLY CORRECT
AND NOT SUITABLE FOR
KIDS UNDER 13

101 THINGS
that piss me off
EXPLETIVES FROM BEHIND CLOSED DOORS

Copyright © 2016
by Georgene Summers (Author)

Along Came Mary Press Publisher

Library of Congress Cataloging

First Publisher: 2017
All Rights Reserved. This book or parts thereof may not be reproduced in any form without written permission of the Author, except for the inclusion of brief quotations in a Review.

ISBN: 978-0-9727920-5-9

Get my Free Newsletter and learn more about my Relationship Coaching Programs at: http://www.aworld4women.com

WARNING:

This Book Is Not Politically Correct And Not Suitable For Anyone Mentally or Physically Under 13

Introduction To The Things That PISS Me Off!

Let's face it, every day we head out on our way to work or the supermarket or some other important place and shit happens that makes us **furious**. If you really tell the truth, you probably wish you had some Ray Gun that would disintegrate some of the rude people that roam the streets, on foot and in cars. Or perhaps, you dream of a Desert Storm Hummer, that would crush that tailgater or speeding maniac, leaving only a grease spot on the asphalt.

We've all been there! Standing in line at the bank while the tellers chat it up. There you are waiting for hours at home for the service technician, who still hasn't arrived. Where the hell is he?

Or maybe you are just sitting on the phone listening to robo-voice direct you to press 1 for this and 2 for that, or she tells you she doesn't understand. Screaming kids, rude Customer Service, packages delivered to the wrong address. I am sick to death of it, aren't you?

Don't you secretly wish you had a special vaporizing

machine for that car that is tailgating you? Hasn't it ever occurred to you to sideswipe the guy who just cut you off going 10 mph? Don't you wish you could put those screaming kids at the other table into a time out? How about saying to the guy with the shopping cart full of stuff in the line marked 12 items only, hey buddy, get the hell out of this line right now?

I am not a complainer! Really! But when I see shit happening, I am the first person to open my mouth and scream out that *pisses me off*!

My blood is boiling and I am compelled to be the voice of reason for all of us who have suffered these 101 gripes or some of these 101 gripes and can relate and perhaps take solace in the fact that we all are the victims. I am not trying to be politically correct and I feel 100% certain, there are things here that will make you angry, pissed off, even annoyed, but they are real, so I say, so what? Now, we can be pissed off, together!

To add some fuel to the fire, I challenge you to send me the things that piss you off and I will include them in my next book, "101 MORE Things That Piss Me Off, Expletives From Behind The Bathroom Door."

So strap yourself in and get ready for a ride into the world of the Rude, Hopeless, Lazy, Self-Centered, Mindless, Thoughtless People of our Country. Buckle up, you're in for a bumpy ride!

NOTE:

There are a number of categories in this book, like Driving, Technology, The Rude, Customer Service and more, and I have shined a light on them on special pages, however, I have not put the things that piss me off into those categorized areas, so just cruise around, have a few laughs, note the different categories, and just enjoy the ride.

My Head Is Exploding and I'm PISSED Off At:

Customer Service

"Who The Hell Is Minding The Store, Damnit?"

1.
PRESSING ONE FOR ENGLISH WHEN I CALL A COMPANY CUSTOMER SERVICE
NEWS FLASH:

What the hell is going on here? This is America, we speak English here. So why must 1 press one for English? When I last looked, I didn't have to press 1 for French in France, or 1 in Spain for Spanish. It should be presumed that you would not have to select the language of the Country you are living in.

We are trying to make English the National language and yet thoughtless companies, like you, ask us to select English to negotiate our way around your annoying, voice activated systems.

Well, I for one am staging a one-person revolt. This idea is just plain wrong and totally Un-American. I refuse to press 1 for English, so put that in your pipe and smoke it. I am just going to stop buying your products. How about that? At some point you will get the message loud and clear and in English, when your products stop selling.

2.
NON-ENGLISH SPEAKING PEOPLE ANSWERING THE CUSTOMER SERVICE PHONES

CUSTOMER SERVICE

I am in the USA. Hello, English spoken here. So, why the Hell is it that almost every time I call Customer Service, for any company, I end up in India or Brazil, Thailand or Guatemala, with someone on the other end of the phone, who hardly speaks English? I feel like a blithering idiot. I have to repeat myself 10 times before you understand what I am saying. Why do I have to pronounce each word as if I am teaching class in a foreign country? Why do I have to ask if you understand why I'm calling? You are Customer Service and I am a Customer! I called a company that was in Indiana. So please, pray tell me, how the hell did I end up in Mombasa?

Why am I discussing a Television Repair issue with a chick in the Philippines? How about we stop exporting our jobs to Customer Service rooms halfway around the world and have English as a requirement for all Customer Service Reps?

101 Things That PISS Me Off

3.
TRUCK DRIVERS THAT TAILGATE.

DRIVING

Listen dude, right now I have your headlights in the trunk of my car, so what the hell is up? I know you are on your way someplace super-important and that you have a load of firearms that need to get to Kansas on time. But I am on my way someplace too and I don't need you in my trunk.

You are 25 times the size of my car and now I can see the color of your contacts in my rear view mirror. When that happens, I know one thing for sure, you are too damn close! I also have to get somewhere in a time frame and I don't want to arrive in a tea cup.

If your goal is to scare me into submission, you win. I'm afraid! I will happily move over, but you are too damned close for me to even do that.

This is one time I wish I had some sort of laser beam that would mysteriously appear from inside my trunk and **Zap** you into a grease spot on the highway.

4.
VOICE ACTIVATED DIRECTIVES FROM COMPANIES

CUSTOMER SERVICE

Hello, hello, LIVE PERSON wanted! Who the hell are you anyway? I am not going to talk to a robot! Someone please tell me: What the hell has happened to Good Old Fashioned Customer Service?

You know, Customer Service, that antiquated idea? It's that smiling person at the end of the phone that makes your company different from any other company. You shipped them off to India or Taiwan or the Philippines. So, guess what? I don't like you anymore.

I am taking my business elsewhere. Just this morning I had to spend 40 minutes on the phone arguing with a machine. A machine! I am paying for a service and you are making me push numbers, during an endless round of questions from a robot. Damnit, I want a live person. There are no live people anymore, only dead people and machines. I want Customer Service and what do I get?

I'll tell you! I get "Yolanda Squat pump," your friendly robotic voice. It's probably the CEO's mother.

I'm told to Press 1 for this and 2 for that and 3 for something else and 9 to repeat the entire damn thing all over again. I don't want any of these things and I don't want her. I curse and she sends me back to the Main Menu. I sneeze and she tells me she didn't understand. Of course, she didn't understand, she isn't human.

MY SOLUTION:

The robot answers, I scream into the phone and continue screaming until "it" gives up in desperation and transfers me to a LIVE person. Profanity also works and truthfully, I find it to be most satisfying.

5.
WATER FAUCETS IN BATHROOM SINKS THAT REQUIRE A MAGIC WAND TO WORK
DEVICES

I have always said "If it ain't broke, don't fix it!" However, that statement falls on deaf ears in Public Restrooms. What the hell did you do with the handles on the water faucets? I ask you, was this something that didn't work? Was this something that cost you money to keep?

I would guess that they worked for decades and that they were cost effective, as handles go. Now I am faced with the following dilemma: I have just left the bathroom and am urged by my own personal cleanliness, as well as signs everywhere, that caution me to wash my hands thoroughly. I step in front of the handle-less sink and stick my hands in front of it, to the side of it, over it, all around it but nothing happens. Not a drip, not a squirt, not a dribble.

The woman next to me with the small child is still holding her up with one hand, trying to wave the faucet into action with the other. She has failed.

So much for reminding your kids to always wash their hands. Another woman walks to the sink and smartly waves her hands under the faucet and presto water, so I know there must be some special code that makes this work. I ask, but she doesn't speak English. Here's my question: why the hell must I have a code or some magical powers to get the bloody faucet to provide water to me in a Public Restroom? It never used to be that way.

Just last month, I used a Public Toilet, read the signs that said wash your hands, turned on the faucet and got water. So what the hell gives now? I'm waving and praying and waving some more and zip, nada, niente, nothing. No water, no dove emerging from the faucet, nothing. I want something! Fix it! Give me back my handles. It's easy, right for cold, left for hot. How hard is this? Stop trying to improve on something that already works. I have a better idea, try improving things that don't work.

6.
FRIENDS WHO SEND FORWARDED CHAIN E MAIL
E-MAIL

OMG, there you are again. I know we are friends, but frankly, I am about to **UN-friend** you. I don't care that I will be facing eternal damnation if I don't forward your chain e-mail to 20 friends immediately. I am willing to take that chance.

I have a lot of things that I do every single day and forwarding your ridiculous e-mail is not at the top of my list. Surely you must have something better to do than e-mail me every other day with promises of Angels and found money. If you don't;

- Get a hobby.

- Buy a dog or a cat.

- Get a turtle or a parrot.

- Take a vacation.

- Play one of those online games, but don't invite me to join you.

Please, I know you love me and want me to be shepherded by Angels for the rest of my days, or for me to have that one special wish granted by the Universe. I will just take my chances, so please don't be offended and just leave my name off of your e-mail list.

7.

DELIVERY COMPANY DRIVERS WHO LEAVE YOUR PACKAGES WHEREVER THE HELL THEY WANT

WORKPLACE

FLASH TO DELIVERY GUYS:

Those odd looking things to the right of the garage door are called steps. The flat thing at the very top is called a porch. Today, I found an urgent overnight letter from my Brokerage Company, buried in the snow in front of my garage. Yes, that was the one with the now destroyed check inside. Last month, you left a box from Neimans' in the middle of some trees, on the neighbor's property.

OMG, do you know that a Gorilla could actually be trained to take that package in his hairy arms, amble up those 4 or 5 steps to the porch and leave it there? That ape would then amble back down, climb into the car and IF he or she could drive, would then leave. **End of story.**

NEWS FLASH! Your drivers hate their job! Clearly they are in the wrong seat on the bus. Yes, the tracking number on your website says DELIVERED, Left at back door. The only problem is, your driver left it at someone elses' back door!

By the way, that box you just threw over the fence is from Dell and just might be a computer! Is it that they can't read? Perhaps they never passed English 101. One would think they could read, but it's probably in another language.

That overnight envelope that you left out in the rain on a wall is probably a check or important documents and could be ruined. But do you care? Of course you don't, because if you did, you would think before you throw.

I say hire Gorillas instead, they do better work, ask for less money and don't sleep on the job. They don't take maternity leave, paid vacations or sick leave. Just teach them how to drive, make sure they have enough fruit, leaves and seeds, sing them a lullaby each night and you will end up with a great worker, who loves their job.

8.
SECURITY TAGS LEFT IN CLOTHING DEVICES

I have just gotten home from shopping, excited to try on my brand new, black silk pants and there it is, staring me in the face: A huge, plastic security tag. It's just stuck into the side of my new pants.

Didn't you look, before you shoved them into that bag? Obviously not! I was going to wear them tonight. Now what? Is it so difficult to check out my new pair of pants before you give them to me, or are you too busy sexting or texting your latest hook-up?

By the way, I don't really know how well your security system is working, because I got all the way home with my pants, complete with security tag fastened tightly onto the seam. No alarms went off when I left the store and there it is, a gigantic plastic apparatus on the leg.

So, I grab the pliers and try to remove this device. I seize it and twist and turn. No luck. Now, I get the big guns by way of a hammer and chisel and begin to slam the device once, twice, three times. By now I am screaming mad.

101 Things That PISS Me Off

You, on the other hand, have a little machine that easily takes this thing off with one swipe of your hand. I am slamming it with a hammer, but nothing is happening. The device is still embedded. A thief would be better prepared than I am.

I know why you didn't see this device. You were too busy texting your boyfriend. Finally, I get it off in pieces, but I have now damaged my pants in the process.

101 Things That PISS Me Off

MEMO TO SALESGIRLS:

- Lay down your cellphone. Your boyfriend will wait, he isn't working.

- Now, check the clothing out totally before you pack it.

- Remove the Security Device

- Pack the item into a bag

- Pick up your cellphone

That way dear, I won't have to use a hammer and chisel to remove the device, or take them to the seamstress for an emergency repair, before they can be worn.

Dude, I'm Seeing Red Over

The Rude

9.
PEOPLE WHO USE THEIR CELLPHONES TO TEXT WHILE DINING WITH FRIENDS AND FAMILY
THE RUDE

Hey you! Yes you, the one with the cellphone attached to your face! I invited you for dinner and guess what? You've got your face glued to your damned cellphone and you're texting. What the hell could be so life-altering that you can't wait until we've eaten to handle it? Is this a matter of life and death?

If it isn't, then put the bloody phone back in your pocket. Did you suddenly become CEO of some company while I wasn't looking? Maybe someone died and left you a huge inheritance and you need to sign transfer documents right now. If neither of those are true, stop texting!

Are you kidding me? I am probably going to be stuck with the bill, because you don't even have a job slinging burgers. So, here's my suggestion: bloody well put down your cellphone and have an adult conversation with me and the other people at our table.

There is nothing you need to be doing that is so important that you can't knock it off while we eat. If there is, then attend to it AND while you are at it, **Pay The Bill.**

10.

PEOPLE TALKING IN MOVIES

THE RUDE

FLASH! You are not at home in your living room. Look around! This is a movie theater. People actually **PAY** to come inside, sit in an uncomfortable seat in the freezing cold, and watch a movie on a big screen. In case you don't get it, people come to see AND hear the movie.

I don't really care what your Aunt Ophelia said to Uncle Oscar this morning, nor do I care if you and your significant other are having a bad day. Go home and fight. Go outside and dump on him, but spare me. Frankly I don't give a damn. I care less about you than I do about the people on the screen and they're just actors.

MEMO TO RUDE THEATER GOERS:

Go home, put on a torn tee-shirt, stick some popcorn in the microwave, add salt and butter to taste. Then flip on the old Zenith, grab a beer or two, some pillows from the bed, honker down and talk as much as you like. That definitely works for me.

One more thing, don't sit behind me and kick my seat. I am not a football. If you must kick something go home and kick your cat, your kid or the neighbors' kid. I don't care. Just stop kicking my seat, it's pissing me off.

11.

DRIVERS WHO PULL OUT IN FRONT OF YOU GOING 10 MILES PER HOUR

DRIVING

What the hell are you doing? You, in the 2002 Toyota with the rusted-out rear panels. Are you blind or just rude? Do you know you just pulled out right in front of me and you are driving like the proverbial little old lady from Pasadena? Did the invisible shield on my truck suddenly inflate without my knowledge?

I guess because it's invisible, how would I know? But you, yes you, in that bright yellow car, you know. I know that because you pulled out in front of me without signaling, when you were only going 10 miles an hour. Obviously, the invisibiity shield was deployed. There is no other explanation.

You must not have seen me, otherwise, why would you do such a stupid thing? Do you have some sort of death wish? I could have hit your bloody car and demolished it totally. Then what?

Oh, I know, you would have cried foul and said I came out of nowhere. You probably don't even have insurance! What is wrong with you? Learn how to drive! Here's the deal;

Driving 101, Try signaling; speeding up or slowing down; Once you make the move, do something, like hitting the gas.

12.

PEOPLE WHO GET INTO EXPRESS LANES AT THE SUPERMARKET THAT SAY 12 ITEMS OR LESS WITH A SHOPPING CART FULL OF STUFF

A BASKET FULL OF HOPELESS

Hey you! Can't you read? Or is it that you just don't give a damn? This is simple Mathematics. The sign says 12 Items or LESS so that means, no more than 12 items.

It does not mean that you can get into that line with your shopping cart filled to the brim with groceries, nor does it mean you can have 20 items. It means that when the sign is lit up, as it is, you may only check out with 12 items or less.

Get out your portable adding machine, or your Smartphone and add the items in your cart. Alternatively, learn to count with your fingers and do it before you get in line.

Which brings me to another winning type of person.

13.

SHOPPERS IN SUPERMARKETS WHO HOLD UP THE LINE WHILE THEY "RUN" BACK TO GET SOMETHING THEY FORGOT.

THE RUDE

Where the hell is your list anyway? There you are in the checkout line and the cashier is totaling up your purchases, when suddenly you realize, **OMG,** you forgot something. Can't you see the line behind you? Are you blind and inconsiderate or just inconsiderate? Instead of checking out and then going back into the market to get that something else, YOU leave the register and the customers, who are in line behind you and run back to find the thing YOU forgot. Sometimes, you even send your 8 year old to "find" that something. There are words for someone like you: rude, thoughtless, selfish, self-centered. to name just a few.

Since you don't seem to get it, this is what you should be doing next time you "forget" while in the checkout line. Pay your bill. Then go back, get the "forgotten" item, stand in line and pay for it. It's called courteous!

Why the hell should I have to stand there waiting for you to get back with your purchase? Next time, make a list and check it twice because otherwise, I might just get **NAUGHTY** and just start screaming at you.

14.
MOLDED PLASTIC COVERING ON STORE ITEMS THAT YOU NEED A BLASTING CAP TO REMOVE.

DEVICES

I have just purchased a package of self-adhesive labels and I want to remove them from the molded plastic container. I look for a tab or an arrow and there is nothing. I grab the scissors, but the plastic is too hard. I break a nail.

Now, I'm pissed off! I grab a hammer, a knife and the scissors to try and accomplish a feat that a 5 year old should be able to handle. That fails to work and threatens to ruin the scissors. I bang my finger with the hammer and cut my hand with the knife.

I call my husband and ask him to bring the heavy machinery. He gets the guillotine! I have nearly destroyed the item and my hand with my futile attempts to get it open. What's the deal here? These are paper labels or maybe they are the label maker.

There is nothing dangerous in here, yet you package this item as if it were solid gold. I get protection, but not from the customer. I get stopping theft, but I bought this and I would like to remove it, in one piece. Yes, I get childproof, but you have gone too far and made this adult proof.

Someone, please tell me why the hell you have to make packaging impervious to those who buy it and would like use the product inside and not just sit and stare at it?

15.

PEOPLE WHO LEAVE THEIR CELLPHONES ON IN MOVIES

THE RUDE

Hey, you in the next row! You've got your bloody cellphone on! What the hell is so important that you need your cellphone on at the movies? Are you expecting a call from the President? Maybe your lawyer telling you the million dollar settlement has just come through? Your ex-wife is phoning to say she is moving to Brazil and you don't have to pay support any longer?

I don't know why the hell you can't wait and allow your phone to take a message. It does that you know. It actually takes messages.

The movie is starting and it's only 2 hours long. Get a grip! The world is not going to spin off its' axis if you don't answer right now. I on the other hand might just grab your phone and throw it into the nearest wall. Or maybe we could test its' waterproof case and toss it into the nearest toilet. How about that?

The huge screen in front of you announces "we don't interrupt your phone call, don't interrupt our movies." Can't you read? Oh I know, you are too busy checking your emails to bother watching the big screen.

Very big people come to the movies too and they can get very angry when you interrupt what they came to see. Lots of very bad things can happen and no one wants to see blood and guts off screen. So, memo to rude, thoughtless, jerk in the next row: Turn off your cell phone or stay the hell home.

16.

PEOPLE WHO ANSWER THEIR CELL PHONES IN THE MOVIES

THE RUDE

Are you kidding? We are in a movie theater and there you are cellphone in hand ready to answer it. It appears as if you are waiting for a phone call. **WHAT?** What the hell is so important that it can't wait? It rings and you answer and begin to chat, it's just like home. Get out of your seat and go to the lobby NOW. This is one time when I wish I had a Death Ray Gun that would vaporize you and your phone.

Apparently you are not only rude, you are deaf too! Didn't you hear the booming voice on the screen tell you to turn off your cellphone? No, you were too busy chatting. You don't care. You are such a jerk that your phone probably burps or farts, instead of ringing like a normal phone. Maybe you have one of those irritating R2D2 Star Wars rings.

Memo To Rude, Possibly Hearing Impaired Theater Goer:

You are not in your living room. You are not even in the lobby of the theater. You are inside, talking, while a movie that folks have paid $15.00 each to see, is playing. No one cares about you or your problems. Take them outside or face the consequences of an upset audience. Life as you know it will not end. Take your chat fest to the lobby. It might if you don't'.

17.
AUTOMATIC PAPER TOWEL DISPENSERS IN BATHROOMS THAT DON'T WORK

DEVICES

What the hell happened to that smart little wheel on the side of the paper towel dispenser in the Public Restrooms? I have no bloody idea, but the replacement is a pain in the ass, excuse the pun. I don't for the life of me understand, what was wrong with the dispenser, which allowed you to turn a dial and bring out a piece of paper towel, so you could dry off your hands. I understand the need to save the trees, I really do and that is why you have those annoying, painfully loud, hand dryers everywhere. However, some Restrooms actually have paper towels.

Sadly, they have begun requiring the user to have some magic password or spell in order to access them. The drawing on the unit clearly shows hands waving across the front and presto, paper towels appear. I waved and I waved again, under, over, in a circle. I then resorted to pleading, begging, threatening. I finally hit the front and still nothing, so I left the restroom with wet hands.

Is this your solution to saving the trees? Please say no! I think I get it! You only have that dispenser there to make people think they will use a proper towel to dry their hands.

Actually, there is nothing inside of that wall ornament. Save the trees, trick the consumer. Force them to either be blown out of the restroom with the blow dryer, or leave with wet hands. Great thinking.

I've Got My Bitch Up About Drivers!

Driving

"I'm Still Pissed Off At What You Did Last Week! So Back Off DUDE!"

18.
DRIVERS WHO IGNORE STOP SIGNS AND RED LIGHTS

DRIVING

FLASH: Elementary School 101: RED means STOP and GREEN means GO. You, in the Red SUV, you ran the hell right through that red light. Cars were at a standstill, as you barreled through. Are you kidding me? To all of you drivers who decided that RED means go, I have a **Newsflash** for you. The opposite is true, it means stop. Children are taught that in grade school! Just because there are only 3 streets at that intersection or no one is approaching to your right, you can't drive through the red light or roll through that stop sign.

  STOP means just that. Pull up and come to a complete, not rolling, but complete and total stop. I hope to hell you have insurance, dude. One of these times, you are going to race through that red light and boom, someone is going to smash into you. The **Good News** is you will then have days or weeks in a hospital bed, getting some basic training on the difference between Red and Green.

So, once again, for those with learning disabilities, **RED** means STOP, **GREEN** means GO. Get it?

19.
PEOPLE WHO PARK IN HANDICAPPED ZONES THAT ARE NOT HANDICAPPED, EXCEPT MENTALLY.

THE RUDE

Hey idiot, can't you see that handicapped sign on the parking spot you just drove into? Funny, I don't see a handicapped permit on your car. Are you blind or just stupid? I know one thing about you…yes you…the person who has just jogged into the convenience store for a pack of cigarettes. You aren't handicapped, but you are a selfish, self-centered, lazy, indolent jerk.

Admittedly, you may be mentally handicapped, but there apparently isn't a permit for that. You should have a sign that indicates Caution, Lazy Driver On Board. There is a parking place for lazy people 50' to your right. When I last checked there wasn't a sign for the mentally handicapped, which would be you. If I were you, I would immediately contact my Congressman and petition to have one made. If that's not an option, then park in the right place and walk you lazy bum.

20.
DRIVERS WHO TURN FROM THE WRONG LANE
DRIVING

Drivers Education 101: There are four directions one can go while driving. Forward, Backward, Right and Left. If you are a helicopter, you can also go up and down. When you are in the right hand lane, you do not get to turn left. When you are in the left hand lane, you do not get to turn right. This is elementary stuff. Did you not learn that when you took your Driving Test? Obviously NOT!

Let me tell you what happens when you do such a stupid, inconsiderate thing. If you bothered to look in your rear view mirror, you would see that you have now blocked traffic in both lanes, while everyone waits for you to cut in front of the guy, turning from the correct lane. It's simple really. This is not rocket science. I am not asking you to send a ship to the moon or to redirect traffic on the 405.

101 Things That PISS Me Off

When you need to make a left hand turn, get into the left turn lane. I assume you do know right from left. If you need to turn right, do not back up traffic, as you bully your car into the right lane, cut someone off, then turn right.

Go straight, turn left, whatever the hell you need to do, but don't block traffic just because you don't know right from left. Try going straight, you know what that looks like I presume, then U turn and go back and do it right. Alternatively, get in the **CORRECT** lane in the first place!

21.
DRIVERS WHO CUT YOU OFF DRIVING

What the hell are you doing? You just cut me off as if I wasn't there. That's me in the third lane, in the black truck. You can't run over me, I'm not your wife! What are you thinking? Am I invisible? Do you not see my black truck right there in that lane next to you?

If you don't, then I have one word for you: Optometrist! If you do, then I have another word for you: Idiot! You could signal, but you don't. You could wait, but you don't.

Sometimes I wish I had a regulation Desert Storm Hummer, that could roll the hell over you, just like you rolled over me, as if I was invisible. Next time dude, use your turn signals first, that's them on the steering wheel and look where you're driving.

22.

PEOPLE WHO PARK AT AN ANGLE AND TAKE UP TWO SPACES

THE RUDE

Hey you, yes you. The one who is now taking up TWO, count them, TWO parking spaces in the crowded parking lot. Do you not see the clearly marked white lines? Are you blind or is it that you just don't give a damn?

I don't care that you have an SUV the size of a drivable RV. Get a smaller car. Get fitted for glasses. Take a course in Driver Etiquette. Can't you see that you have now taken up two spaces?

One day, someone with a bigger truck, is going to pull in right next to you, close enough to hear you breathe. Then, they are going to open their heavy duty door right into the side of your new car. **Boo Hoo, Parking Hog.**

Suffice it to say there is a special place for you people… and it's not in Heaven.

23.
TRYING TO FIND THE END OF A NEW ROLL OF TOILET PAPER IN A DISPENSER IN A PUBLIC TOILET

WORKPLACE

Memo To Maintenance Workers: Restroom maintenance is not Rocket Science. I am not asking you to write a paper on the Magna Carta nor am I requesting that you be able to provide the solution to World Hunger. I am merely asking you to find the beginning of the toilet paper roll, BEFORE you slap it into that impenetrable contraption that hangs on the wall.

So here I am sitting on the toilet and I cannot find the start of the roll. I am digging, scratching and tearing before finally pulling off a chunk of paper far too small to do any good at all.

My choices now are to waddle with a wet bottom to the next stall, provided no one else in the bathroom at the time or to pray that someone is in the stall next to me and ask them for some toilet paper. Neither is a good solution.

The real solution is for you to locate that little end prior to installing it into that impermeable wall-hanging device. It can't be that hard. Just roll it until you see that extra end and then pull it out. Now place the toilet paper roll in the wall device and close. Thanking you in advance.

24.

IDENTITY THIEVES

A BASKET FULL OF HOPELESS

Yes, I know that Identity Thieves have eyes in the back of their heads and that I need a service to protect me, but why? You, Mr. or Miss Freaking, no-account, lame-assed, Identity thief, should get a bloody job like everyone else! But no, you don't want to do that. You would rather lurk around ATM's, installing special machines to steal my pin and my money. You just want to slither around in the dead of night, like some slimy night-crawler and steal my credit card details so you can buy that airline ticket to Ethiopia, a $600.00 motorcycle part or new dress. God knows you could probably use one, even if it's just to dine out at your favorite Fast Food spot.

101 Things That PISS Me Off

There's no denying you're good at what you do, **stealing!** Every day you find another way to steal from some person or company. You are nothing but a low life snake.

You could take your talent to new heights and go to work for a security company building firewalls. There I said it, the W word. But no not you!

You are a lazy bum and a thief. You could wait tables at some restaurant, even stuff envelopes at home. But no, not you. You probably used to hold up little old ladies for their Supermarket coupons. Thanks to you, I suspect everyone. I scrutinize the waitress as she walks away with my credit card. Is she secretly taking a picture of it?

I know you don't give a damn how long it takes for me to clean up the credit mess that your theft caused. I will tell you anyway, years. Thank you very much. Personally I hope you rot in hell. There is a very special place in the world for all of you, JAIL!

25.
CREDIT REPORTING COMPANIES
A BASKET FULL OF HOPELESS

Excuse me! I'm talking to you, the overpaid, underworked person at the Credit Reporting Company. Pay attention. What made you decide that I was the John Smith who declared bankruptcy in 1990? Here I am trying to get a home loan and I'm told no way and why? It's because you made a negative report about someone and stuck it in my file.

I am not **him**. I am a 40 year old woman and my name is not John, it's Joanna. I live in Indiana not Arizona. I'm single with no kids, not married with 3 kids. I don't own a home, thanks to you nor do I drive a Toyota Truck.

I call Customer Service, but we all know what they end up doing. **Voice Mail Jail** that's what! I hate you! When I finally reach a human, you pause and then tell me it's not your department. So, I ask you, whose department is it and where the hell is the Supervisor?

You put me on hold listening to a bad rendition of Who Let The Dogs Out and leave me, never to return again. After an enduring 15 minutes, I realize you are not coming back and hang up.

101 Things That PISS Me Off

This is all your fault. Why the hell can't you recognize the difference between a Joanna and a John and Indiana and Arizona? Perhaps you are not a human after all. Perhaps you are just another stupid machine.
I still hate you.

If Bitching Isn't Your Thing, To Hell With You...

I Hate SPAM!

"One Day I'm Going To Find You and Then All HELL Is Going To Break Loose!"
"I Hate SPAM!"

26.
BUSINESS PEOPLE WHO ARE NEVER AT THEIR DESKS WHEN YOU CALL.

CUSTOMER SERVICE

One Ringie Ding, Two Ringie Dings, Three Ringie Dings. So where are you now? What the Hell are you doing? You have a job and it doesn't include travelling around the office. You don't even have a Passport! You are in Customer Service, but for the life of me I don't' see any of that going on. It used to be that people were at their desks servicing their customers.

Only a few years ago, one could call and an actual Human would answer the phone. Today, that is a novel, almost unheard of idea! What I want to know is where the Hell are you? You are being paid to work, so why aren't you at your desk? You can't be spending all day at the water cooler or in the restroom, or can you? Excuse me for saying this, but I just want to call and have you pick up the phone and help me. Is that so wrong? I don't think so. Here's the thing: if you can't be at your bloody desk during working hours, at least leave some loving message on your voice mail that makes me feel all warm and fuzzy!

27.
COMPUTERS OUR SAVIORS
TECHNOLOGY

NOT! Paperless society my Ass! I want you to check out this slew of documents, piled high on my desk. They are back up for an erratic machine called the computer. I am absolutely not paperless. I am a trapped human, tied to a machine that can be totally unreliable, relentlessly unforgiving and keeps us buried in documents we fear losing, if that thing we covet crashes. Sound familiar?

Sure, back it up to another technological device. I ask you, just what the hell is the Cloud and does anyone know where it is? I mean, it's a freaking Cloud somewhere in outer space. Some people I know still use the old, totally reliable yellow lined legal pad. Remember that? It works just fine. Oh, excuse me, I have to go, my computer just crashed.

28.

PEOPLE WHO SHARE EVERYTHING ON SOCIAL MEDIA

A BASKET FULL OF HOPELESS

I realize that you don't really have a very full and exciting life, seriously, I do. I understand that you spend a lot of your waking hours on Facebook and Twitter and even Instagram and Snapchat. Good for you! I'm sure you see it as being productive. But seriously, do you really think I am interested in knowing that you had a great bowel movement this morning, or that little Billie vomited all over the new couch? If your answer is yes, than you need more help then I thought.

I do want to know how your life is unfolding, but I don't need you to tell me in detail about the fight you had last night with your mother, sister, brother, boyfriend or about your visit to the gynecologist. Really, it's not my business and I am totally uninterested.

You should ask yourself whether sharing your entire life with the world is a good idea. Personally, I think not. Those 558 close friends might one day be frenemies or outright enemies and you have now bared your soul, and in some cases, more than that, to the world of the Internet.

101 Things That PISS Me Off

Since you need a hobby or at the very least something to occupy your time, here are a few novel ideas for you:

- Take up gardening
- Build something. A shed, a wall, a tree house.
- Have an affair, but don't talk about it
- Attend a Yoga class
- Try out Martial Arts
- Collect stamps or rocks, they don't judge or talk
- Get a Job
- Take up cleaning your house as a hobby
- Play bridge with the girls
- Invest in a shrink
- Take a trip to the zoo. You might have something in common with some of the residents.

That will take up the space of losing Social Media as your pastime and provide you with the feelings of accomplishing something other than sharing every detail of your mundane life, with your world of so called friends.

29.

PEOPLE WHO PARK IN NO PARKING ZONES

THE RUDE

Question? Are you blind? Can't you read the signs? Are you not aware that those bright yellow lines that extend from the curb outside the supermarket mean something? The sign on the side of the road screams **FIRE LANE NO PARKING?** But there you are sitting in your car or not, waiting for someone to finish shopping.

Maybe you have just dashed in to the liquor store. Sadly, the fire truck that needs that lane hasn't arrived and demolished your car. There are 100 or more parking places in the lot. You can text all you want while sitting in one of those empty spaces. Not only are you parked illegally, but you are taking up a lane of traffic and causing a traffic jam, you idiot. Move your car. Shame on you!

30.

POLITICIANS

A BASKET FULL OF HOPELESS

No scribe would be complete without a Basket of Politicians. This is a special time of year and I have a question. Where the hell did they find these guys? What a conglomeration of hopeless! Promise after promise followed by more promises, all of which are lies! We know when you're lying, because your lips are moving!

This year, we are being treated to a host of moving lips. Promises made, only to be broken and unchecked, uncharted territory that leaves most of us biting our nails to the quick; waking up in prayer each morning or counting our prematurely gray hairs each night.

WTF I'm voting for the short guy with the mouse ears. Oops, he's not on the ballot! I know this is a unique concept, but how about a time out on the dirty tricks and let's have a clean campaign? How about this Politicos? Let's promise everything and at least deliver something?

31.
SMOKERS WHO STAND AND SMOKE AT THE ENTRANCE TO A NON-SMOKING BUILDING

SMOKERS

I have just come up with a new business and one that can thrive in any city, Oxygen Masks! You have got to love this guy or gal. You, the smoker, works in a non-smoking building, but there you are, standing right outside the front doors, smoking. Clearly, this is so you can share the joy as others leave the building. Why do I have to cover my mouth and nose with a cloth when departing a building? I shouldn't have to, but there you are, leaning against the wall encased in a cloud of nicotine filled smoke.

I gasp as the smoke slithers into the open door and the smoke-free building. I hold my breath, but it's no use. I can only see a vague outline of you in the smoke as I rush to get away. Listen up! I quit by choice. I am no longer a fan of cancer sticks and I don't need you to be sharing your joy. You are the minority because most people who can read, have already quit. Smoking stinks and frankly you do too.

Memo To Smoker: that Skull and Crossbones on the outside of each package indicates DANGER. You are in Danger! But then so am I! I don't really care if you smoke yourself to death. Just do it on your own.

Drop your cigarette and back away from the building. I am tired of holding my breath as I rush past you gagging. Hey, I have an idea! Maybe you should be locked in a room without windows for a week. It's the new high tech way to quit.

32.

PEOPLE WHO DON'T PUT THEIR SHOPPING CARTS BACK INTO THE HOLDING AREA

THE RUDE

I understand that you are above this sort of plebian activity, but hear this. The parking lot at King Kullen is not a storage area for abandoned shopping carts. The one that you just left sitting empty in the middle of the Supermarket lot is magnetically attracted to other things metal, like cars and will probably slam into one with the slightest provocation.

101 Things That PISS Me Off

A strong wind or a careless, or not so careless shove from another lazy patron and Oops, $1000.00 worth of damage to your canary colored Hummer in an instant.

One day that might even be your car, but for the time being it isn't. I know this because you have already driven off. I realize that taking your empty shopping cart 25 feet to that cart holding area is hard work. I get it!

Well toughen up Mister, because I am sick to death of lazy people like you. Take your empty bloody cart and put it one of two places: either back in the cart area or shove it into your trunk and take it home.

One day the winds are going to be blowing up a storm and some idiot just like you is going to have left an empty cart in the parking lot and while you are mindlessly navigating your way through the produce aisle, that empty cart is going to be navigating its way into your car. So try that on for size. Put your carts away you lazy fool.

33.

DRIVERS WHO CHAT ON THEIR CELLPHONE WHILE DRIVING

DRIVING

Are you crazy? You are on a Highway going 80 mph and chatting it up as if you were sitting in a reclining chair in your living room. I glance over as you race past me and there you are chatting away, phone in one hand, cigarette in the other. I have no idea what is holding onto the wheel, but off you go, speeding in front of me and frankly, it's making my hair turn grey.

Are you insane or just stupid? Who the hell are you talking to anyway? Your Parole Officer? Your Mistress? Your Mother? Where is that police officer when you need him? There are laws against what you are doing in every state in the land. Either you don't give a damn or you can't read, maybe both. I think it's that you don't really give a rat's ass. This is one time when I wish I was a cop so I could nail your ass and write you the biggest reckless driving ticket ever. Baring that: here's a suggestion: Pull the hell over and chat or get Blue Tooth.

33A.
DRIVERS THAT TAILGATE
DRIVING

Good Day to the car currently attached to my bumper! The measure that I have of whether you are too bloody close or not is: Can I see your license plate in my rear view mirror or not? If it's OR NOT, back off!. But you don't. Ten miles later and there you are, glued to my bumper. Do you know what you are? A BULLY!. You are manic in your pursuit and focused in trying to force me into another lane, even though I am driving faster than the well-posted speed limits.

Can't you read? The sign says 65 and I am already going 73, but you stay attached to me like some kind of flesh eating parasite. You are a possessed, manic moron behind the wheel of a 5000 pound killing machine. You could go around, but you don't because you just love pushing people around.

You probably snatch shopping carts from little old ladies and rip candy out of the mouths of kids. You are that guy who trips the disabled person stepping off the curb and probably puts up a street barricade when a blind person is crossing.

101 Things That PISS Me Off

The lane next to me has room for your oversized ego machine, but you stay attached to my trunk hoping to make me succumb. Listen dude, you are so close that I can't even move over. I already don't like you so here is what I am going to do. I am going to slow down to the speed limit. I am not going to give in to your bullying ways. I will drive at 65 mph until you go around me I tap the brakes and you freak out. I tap them again and watch as the blood drains from your face. Yes, you are that close.

I am not intimidated by the Alaska State salute that you provide as you finally pull around. I have met bullies before and I am sure I will again. Here YOU are and it's just Monday morning. My satisfaction comes from the knowledge that one day a cop will be hiding in a bush and see you speeding along the highway, tailgating and he will track you down and ticket you.

You will probably give him some grief and he will end up handcuffing you and carting your ass off to jail. Maybe I will be lucky enough to pass you by and shout obscenely at you while waving the Alaska State Salute. You are a sorry sight in handcuffs. There is absolutely no reason for you to be glued to my bumper you idiot, so you can go straight to Hell or to Jail. FYI Dude, this IS where Bullying begins and your kids get their first lesson.

34.

DRIVERS WHO DON'T SIGNAL WHEN TURNING

DRIVING

I know your hands are tired from a long day picking corn in the fields, but is it so difficult to push the lever on the steering wheel up or down and indicate you are about to make a turn? It certainly seems to be a challenge to you. Here we are driving happily along and suddenly you stop.

Is there a person walking across the street? Did a deer suddenly leap out in front of you? Did you faint at the wheel? No, you have decided to turn left and I am now sitting behind you, unable to get into another lane. What is the matter with you? Do you have a broken arm? Did you forget you wanted to turn at this junction? Or as I suspect, are you just lazy?

Years ago you needed to put your arm outside the window, rain or shine and make a proper signal before turning left or right. Today all you have to do is push the lever up or down before you turn.

101 Things That PISS Me Off

One of these fine days someone is going to slam into the rear of your car because they didn't "get" that you were turning. As a note of caution you might want to make sure your insurance is current, that your seat belts work properly and that everyone in your car is belted up nicely just in case someone hits you from behind.

Pissed Off Enough Yet, Or Do You Want Some More?

Devices

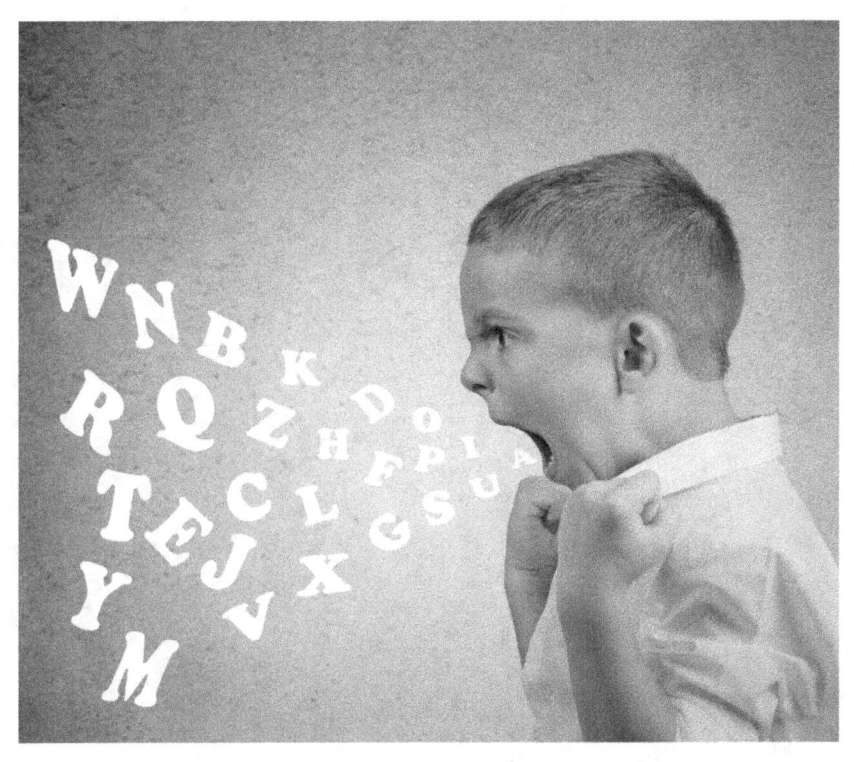

"Can You Hear Me Now? How About Now? Two Tin Cans And A String Worked Better!"

35.

DRIVERS IN THE FAST LANE ON FREEWAYS DRIVING UNDER THE SPEED LIMIT

DRIVING

Are you blind? There must be 10 reflective signs per mile that smartly announce the speed limit. So can't you read? It says 65 not 35. Put your foot on the gas and move it along.

Now I know you are older than the average motorist because I can see you struggling to hold onto the steering wheel and straining to see the highway. It looks like you are sitting on a pillow and there is a blue and white handicapped tag on your rear view mirror. I am totally sympathetic, believe me.

I understand unbridled **FEAR** when I see it. Your knuckles are white and the veins are standing out on your forehead. But, here is the rub. If driving the right speed is a problem, then I would suggest Uber or a Taxi or perhaps you should stay at home. Hitchhike! People will be totally sympathetic to you there as well. On the freeway however, not so much.

36.

DRIVERS WHO DON'T PULL FORWARD AT THE GREEN LIGHT AND THEN SIT THROUGH ANOTHER RED LIGHT

DRIVING

Ho Hum, excuse me! You up there in front of me, in the Yellow SUV! Are you asleep or what? What the hell are you doing up there anyway or dare I ask? You have just sat through the entire green light or arrow. You sat through one complete light and now are ready to sit through another.

Are you blind? Green means **GO**. The intersection is there for you to pull into. You don't need to sit behind the double lines and wait while the green light, which means **GO**, changes to a red light which normally means stop, but in your case still means **GO,** because you should be out in the intersection ready to turn left. Do it!

I know, you are texting or sexting or checking on your stocks. Maybe you are just chatting with your boyfriend, your mother, your shrink, your neighbor. So listen up!

Text and chat all you want, but here are my suggestions: Pull your car into the Walmart lot and text your boyfriend; Pull over on the side and set your hazard lights to blinking and text your mom; Stay home until you have gotten all the texting out of your system for the day. Otherwise bloody pay attention and drive. That is what roads are for, driving. So do it for God's sake.

37.

CONTAINERS WITH LIDS THAT WONT' OPEN

DEVICES

I understand the need to make prescription bottles with a cap that needs to be blasted off, but what is this latest sadistic contraption all about? OMG, what the hell is going on? The vitamin container, please? Are you afraid that I am going to overdose on your gummy vitamins or what? It clearly says twist with little arrows indicating a direction.

I took the jar home and twisted and nothing happened. I pushed, I pulled, I banged, I hit and then I twisted again and still nothing, nada, niente. I cannot take my vitamins if I cannot get to them.

Who in the hell invented this top anyway, some sadistic monster you employ to drive your customers into a nervous breakdown? Well, let me tell you Mr. CEO of this **OhLaLa** Vitamin Company, right now I think YOU are a sadist. How about that?

Do you know what I had to do to get your gummy vitamins open? I returned to the store in the pouring rain and asked the young man at the counter for help. Guess what? He pushed, he pulled, he twisted, he pressed down and he couldn't get them open either.

So bully for you. You invented a cap that no child or adult could open. It took two more salesmen and a manager before, presto, finally opened. I hope you have a Patent for that one!

38.

COMMERCIALS IN MOVIE THEATERS

A BASKET FULL OF HOPELESS

Are you kidding me? I have just taken out a mortgage to pay your outrageous $15.00 movie ticket prices and that's not for 3D folks. If I want a box of popcorn, I have to leave my first born. I must deal with the guy behind me who is kicking my seat and the folks on one side who are chatting up a storm and a kid running up and down the aisles. Now I have to watch a commercial on top of that?

Suddenly there it is, a commercial for a car company or a computer company or the Hair Salon down the road. I can stay home with a glass of wine and some cheese crackers without a screaming kid or chatty neighbors and watch commercials. You get plenty of money from the tickets and the fattening crap you sell at the concession stand. Knock it off with the commercials.

Suggestion:

First, your shrink called to say, get back on your meds. Then ashcan the commercials or lower the ticket prices, or both.

39.
LISTENING TO CORPORATE PROMOTIONAL BULL WHILE ON HOLD IN VOICE MAIL JAIL

CUSTOMER SERVICE

I don't care that you are the greatest company since the dawn of mankind. I am totally not interested in the fact that you think you are providing excellent Customer Service. The truth is, this is anything but that. I think you need to hold off the self-promoting bull with existing customers. I am one of those people and I say **spare me**. I didn't call to hear you sing your praises, robotically, but rather because I have a burning problem and you are it. Frankly, I don't think you're so great.

While you think Delivery is key to your dubious success, you have once again lost my package and you don't know where the hell it is. So here I sit, trapped in Corporate Hell, listening to some ratchet-voiced employee extoll on the virtues of your company. If you were so fabulous I wouldn't be calling. It's bad enough you have me trapped in a version of voice mail jail, but give me a choice and let me tune out of your self-promoting garbage.

40.

EXTREME COUPONERS DOING WHAT THEY DO BEST

A BASKET FULL OF HOPELESS

Yes, of course I realize that this has become something you think is chic, but if I am in line behind you I promise, it is anything but that. I don't really care that you have a Reality Show named after what you do, or that your entire family of 15 spends days haunting neighbor's yards for throw away newspapers. What I do care about is that sometime today, I have to get home and feed my own family and there you are with 6 shopping carts of groceries and an oversized 3-ring binder, crammed with thousands of alphabetized coupons.

Yes, I admire your tenacity and the fact that you are intent on beating your own record by trying to save $474.00 of your $500.00 bill. Whoopee! But here's the problem: you have over 100 cans of dog food and I couldn't help but hear you tell the shocked cashier that you have no dogs.

There is enough shampoo in your carts to wash a village for a year and 50 boxes of Headache remedy.

101 Things That PISS Me Off

The doctor says clipping coupons can give you a migraine, so I get that.

Then there are the 75 bottles of Sprite; 110 boxes of Wet Wipes; 68 Bottles of Room Deodorizer; 105 boxes of Insect Repellent; 43 Jars of Mayonnaise; 73 Bags of Frozen French Fries, 57 boxes of Hair Remover and 103 cartons of low fat yoghurt. I ask myself, what is dinner like at this house?

I envision family members eating fries topped with yoghurt and mayo. I immediately feel nauseous. It's amazing that you can be so dedicated and convince 15 of your family members to spend their days clipping coupons, while you spend your nights organizing them.

All of this so that you can get $500.00 worth of products, most of which you can't eat or use, for $26.00 and 525 hours of work. I, on the other hand, get nothing, but have to stand in line behind you as you dig out coupon after coupon, reducing your bill one item at a time.

Suggestion:

Why not just get a job stuffing envelopes from home. You too can make money and then go wild at the market buying stuff you can actually eat.

41.

THE PEOPLE WHO SAY IT'S NOT MY DEPARTMENT

CUSTOMER SERVICE

It is your department! You are Customer Service, Number 9. I clearly pressed Customer Service, number 9 as instructed by robo-voice. Now you tell me you are not Customer Service after all. So who the hell are you anyway and why are you answering the Customer Service line?

If somehow your company is so lame that you got the extensions mixed up, have someone in that department fix it. You are just too lazy to do the job you are being paid for. I know that minimum wage isn't enough for a stellar worker like you. I mean after all, you actually have a GED and think you should be promoted. Well, you will be, right after you stop passing the buck, answer my question and come up with a solution. I will immediately talk to your boss about that promotion. No promises mind you, but I know which button to press to get **YOUR** Supervisor.

I've Made Bitching An Art Form!

Technology

"You SUCK!"

42.

TAXES

A BASKET FULL OF HOPELESS

I don't get it. I buy my house, which, when I last looked, included the land and you send me a bill for my property! Are you kidding me? You tax my car three times, isn't once enough? Apparently not! I spit in the road and you tax me. I fart and there's a pollution tax.

Just what the hell are you doing for me? Absolutely nothing! I don't have kids in school and frankly, I don't care that you do. I work out of my home, so I am not wearing out the bridges and highways. Speaking of those "highways" what the hell is wrong with the roads in this place? They are a disaster.

I'm retired and haven't had a raise in my Social Security in years and do you care? No! The bills are due July 1 and you send them out June 27 so no one has a chance to storm your office in protest. Why bother, you are on vacation anyway. Lucky you! I don't get a vacation, because my money is paying for property taxes

Have you no shame? Have you no heart? I have just broken the axle to my car on these ruptured things you call roads. Why the hell aren't you spending some of MY tax dollars fixing them? Either that or buy me a ticket to an offshore tax haven so I can hide my money like you do.

43.

PEOPLE WHO WEAR BASEBALL CAPS IN THE MOVIES WITH THE BILLS TURNED UP

A BASKET FULL OF HOPELESS

Hey, dude! You are not at a game. I'm talking to you. The one who just arrived at the near empty theater, baseball cap perched on his head. Yes you, the one who just sat down right in front of me. Like, are there no other seats you could pick? Are you blind and stupid? Then, to make matters worse you flip the bill up. God forbid your view should be obstructed, but now, mine is.

101 Things That PISS Me Off

Take the stupid hat off! What the hell are you covering up anyway?

- Are you bald?

- Are there horns protruding from your head?

- Is your head full of tattoos or crazy piercings?

- Do you have some raging skin disease?

If the answer to some or all of these is no, take your damn hat off!

I just want to slap you across the back of your head and knock that stupid hat off. Even in the worst, most socially deprived areas of our nation, people usually learn manners. As a child you should have learned that you do **NOT** wear your hat inside. That is unless you were raised by wolves. Wear it on your way to wherever, then take it off. Otherwise someone might knock it off.

44.

BUSINESS PEOPLE WHO DON'T CALL BACK WHEN YOU LEAVE A MESSAGE

CUSTOMER SERVICE

I have now left three messages for you and nothing has happened. You are a business, or at least that is what you call yourself. What the hell are you doing all day? I called you and left a message, two days ago and another this morning. What makes you think your time is more valuable than mine? Guess what? It isn't.

Listen up, I am the customer. If it weren't for me you would be home stuffing envelopes   How busy can you be? Put down that bagel, stop texting and call me back. Is it that you don't know how to retrieve your voice mail messages? Take a course! Call your Manager, your sister, your mother. Call someone.

Why do I have to call you again and spend 10 minutes wading through that litany of interactive prompts just to leave you another message? Who the hell are you anyway? I'll tell you who you are not. You are **NOT** the Owner of the company. You are **NOT** the President or CEO. You are just another employee, so have some manners, because guess what? You can be replaced, with a robot.

45.
POOR TO NON EXISTENT CUSTOMER SERVICE
CUSTOMER SERVICE

Hey you! **RED ALERT!** See me? I'm the reason you have a job. I'm a Customer. You do know what that is, don't you? I buy things from your boss. Oh and by the way, that is the optimum word, Boss. This requires no explanation. Just because you work for a Giant in the industry doesn't mean you have to be rude.

But then, you come by it naturally don't you? You know who you are, you Giants of Industry. You are the very same ones who have sent your Customer Service departments to places where people don't speak English. Ok I get it, it's about making money plain and simple, but at least if I have to speak to someone whose first language isn't English, let them understand English.

Try giving them some basic lessons starting with the Customer, that would be me, is always right and that would be correct. While you're at it tell them **NOT** to talk over me. I have called with a monumental problem and your company is the cause, so have them listen and be sympathetic. Please, while you are at it, urge them not to tell me how many other **upset customers** they have had to deal with today.

46.

JUNK MAIL

A BASKETFUL OF HOPELESS

Who the devil are you and how do you find me? Not that I really care anymore. I want you to **un-find** me. Just because somehow you have found out that I am chronologically a Senior, you assume that I need a Hearing Aid; An Assisted Living Home; A Wheelchair; A Life Alert System.

I don't and I don't appreciate the onslaught of mail directing me to call you and take advantage of your Special Offer. My hearing is just fine. I am walking just great, thank you. I haven't fallen, but if I did, I can still get up on my own. I wouldn't dream of going to an Assisted Living Center or a Senior Housing Development, ever.

If I want new auto insurance, I will call my broker. I can still dial a phone. While we're at it, if I want a new phone, I will drive over to the mall and buy one. So, leave me the hell alone.

GASP!
Who The Hell
Hasn't Wanted To
Bitch About This?

Smokers!

"Electronic Cigarettes
My Ass!
I've Had It!
We Are DONE!"

47.
PEOPLE WHO SMOKE WHILE EATING

THE RUDE

Hey you with the yellow fingers! I can tell that your food tastes better with some smoke mixed in, but mine not so much. I am watching as you take a bite and then a puff and then another bite and another puff.

Seriously? Are you kidding? The food must taste like you are eating it out of an ashtray.

Are you so addicted to nicotine that you cannot wait until you finish that slab of overcooked barbequed meat, before you inhale that lung full of smoke? It would be easier and cheaper for you to just chop up a pack of those delicious ciggies, pour some barbeque sauce over them, heat and eat. I'm pretty sure it would taste the same. Just think you wouldn't even have to leave your smoke filled living room.

Doesn't that just sound **Yummy?**

48.

PEOPLE WHO BRING THEIR SMALL CHILDREN TO R RATED MOVIES

THE RUDE

No matter what you think, honey, American Psycho is **NOT** a movie for children. Yes, there is a dog in it. Yes, there are some cute young actors in it too. But, that is where the cuteness ends and scary begins. **Memo To Those Who Are Ratings Deprived:** For those of you who seem not to understand what the Ratings mean, X Rated and R Rated mean no one under the age of 17. Clearly you have read this wrong. This does not mean that you should be bringing your 5 and 6 year old to watch as Christian Bale uses a **Rivet Gun** to murder a young girl or gauges the eyes out of that little dog. It also doesn't mean that you give your 7 year old a History lesson by taking him to see the R-Rated Twelve Years A Slave! Censors are there for a reason. Ratings are on movies so that mental midgets like you know what movies **NOT** to take your children to. I can see that we all underestimated the **stupidity** of some parents. So I guess we now have to card you at the ticket counter.

Here's A Thought: Leave them home with your mother, brother, sister, father's brother twice removed. I don't really give a damn or get Netflix, buy some popcorn; get some sugary sodas and hunker down to watch something with a Kardashian in it.

49.

PEOPLE WHO THROW TRASH OUT OF THEIR CAR WINDOWS

THE RUDE

Who are you? I can't for the life of me imagine what your home looks like. Maybe you are one of those Buried Alive Hoarders that we see on TV who just takes things out of the wrappers and tosses them on the living room floor.

You probably have to dig your way into the kitchen and shower outside using a hose because your trailer is so full of trash. Were you brought up in a barn or do you just behave like you were raised by wolves? Do you think that nobody saw you ditch your junk out the window? We did.

101 Things That PISS Me Off

Your paper bag nearly hit our car. You sped off and thought you were so cool. I've got your number, Hoarder. Dude, you are anything but that. You are a lazy, no account, wrapper hoarding, trailer trashing, hot-dog eating fool. I know because that is some of what you just tossed out your car window. You are a slob! I would bet the farm that your torn tee shirt is stained with catsup and mustard and your hair looks like you just spent a week in a wind machine. You don't give a damn about how you look. I can just imagine how your car looks with a pile of empty pizza boxes, squashed beer cans, food wrappers from the take out joint and empty Styrofoam cups. You are a one man pollution machine. Well better surrounding you than littering up the streets.

50.

HAVING TO WAIT ALL DAY FOR THE SERVICE GUY

CUSTOMER SERVICE

Hello Service Provider, where are you? You were supposed to be here an hour ago. I gave you a window and what did you do with it? You went to lunch. You stopped by your girlfriends' house for a beer. You kicked it at the beach. But here's a question, why do I have to wait for you?

Yes, it used to be a full day hanging around waiting for you to show up to fix something that was your fault. But now you say, morning or afternoon, which still means I have to sit around waiting for you to finish your breakfast or lunch; stop chatting with your last appointment; texting your girlfriend; having a Starbucks or searching for Pokeman creatures in the cemetery and only then, do you get your truck and yourself to my place. I keep asking myself why? Are you **that** important?

It was then that I decided to examine this phenomenon a bit closer. I wondered, are you sleeping with the boss? Are you blackmailing someone in Human Resources? Are you related to the owner by blood? If the answers are no then why aren't you here fixing my TV, delivering my parcel, checking out the cable? You aren't even a Government employee who can't be fired. I don't get it and I don't care to. Just get your sorry ass to my house on time.

51.

PEOPLE WHO SMOKE IN ELEVATORS.

THE RUDE

Are you blind? Did you fail reading classes in Grammer School? Do you not see that sign affixed to the **INSIDE** of the elevator? It's clearly says **NO SMOKING** and it's in three languages, English, Spanish and Chinese. It doesn't say NO SMOKING for everyone except for you. It doesn't say stop smoking **after** you get inside the elevator and then put the cigarette out in a cup or on the floor. It says **NO SMOKING**. You are a pariah in today's society who continues to smoke cancer sticks, ignoring the skull and crossbones that appear on each pack. That in itself says to me that you are totally insane.

I suppose that could explain the fact that you can't read. **Insanity!** A normal person sees a skull and crossbones on any package and it screams don't drink me, don't eat me, don't smoke me, but not you. That tells me either you can't read or you have a suicide wish. Frankly I don't care about either.

Reading classes are held weekly at the local **YMCA**, take one. Get a dictionary and find out what the skull and crossbones means. You already smell like an ashtray, so standing beside you is not pleasant. Please, smoke yourself into oblivion outside or inside your house, but don't pollute the elevator.

52.

DRIVERS WHO HAVEN'T A CLUE WHERE THEY ARE GOING

DRIVING

Hey you! Yes, you in the beaten up 1999 Toyota Truck with the rust consuming the back right panel. You, the one that has 14 I'm A Patriot Bumper stickers all over your car. I am behind you and your turn signal indicating a left turn has gone on and off a dozen times over the past mile and a half. Where the hell are you turning?

Do you even know where you are? You stop and appear to be making a turn, then suddenly you start up again. WTF do you not have GPS in that junk heap? Do you not have a map you can turn to in times of trouble?

I am behind you and don't have a clue what the hell you are doing or where the hell you are going. Believe me dude you are about to be in a whole heap of trouble if you don't make up your mind and turn or go straight. Frankly I don't give a damn which way you go, just do something or pull the hell over and park that pile of junk.

53.

EMPLOYEES WHO REFUSE TO PUT YOU THROUGH TO A SUPERVISOR

CUSTOMER SERVICE

Customer Service, my Ass! If this is service then I am the Devine Light of Guidance in a Sea of Darkness! This is a joke! Listen up employee 267984, who won't give me her last name. I am the Customer here and I have a Customer Service problem. Did you not understand what I just said? I asked for your Supervisor. You just put me on terminal Hold.

Guess what? You are **NOT** the boss. You are quite simply a paid, albeit to hear you tell it, underpaid employee. You do not get to make decisions that impact my life. I have politely asked for a Supervisor. Don't think you can leave me on hold listening to annoying rap music until I finally hang up. I can outlast your music, even the heavy metal crap. Don't think you can pretend to transfer me to a Supervisor and then disconnect me. I already have your name, rank and serial number and I do intend to report you. You can't help me so give me someone who can **Right Now!**

Lazy, Workers Piss Me Off Royally!

Workplace

"Damn Girl, You Used The W Word!"

54.

CUSTOMER SERVICE PEOPLE WHO SAY, "NO ONE ELSE IS GOING TO GIVE YOU ANY OTHER ANSWER. THIS IS FINAL

CUSTOMER SERVICE

OMG who the hell are you to tell me that **you** are the last word? You are making minimum wage, working part-time in a phone bank. Okay, so you may be in the USA but you are **not** the final word. You are not the President of the company. You are not a Supervisor. You are not even in charge of a tiny group of misfits in your section. So who the hell are to say "no one else is going to tell you anything different?" How the hell do you know? You haven't had a raise in 5 years and they still have you putting trash in the shredder at night.

So, say you're sorry and give me to someone with a higher pay grade. While I am happy that you have such a strong view about your own importance, you are not the **final say.** There is someone above you who will be happy when I report your actions to them. If you had the final answer, guess what dude? You would be **CEO!**

55.

PEOPLE WHO GO OUT WEARING THEIR PAJAMAS

A BASKET FULL OF HOPELESS

Are you kidding me? You are clearly over the age of 12 and those are **Shrek pajamas** on your hairy body, and there you are, standing in line at the local Supermarket. Did you just get up? Are you on drugs? Don't you have a full length mirror? Don't you work? Did you somehow forget to get dressed this morning? Well listen up! I don't understand anyone who goes out wearing their pajamas. Caveat being, it's Christmas morning, you are 8 years old, still believe in Santa and are headed over to Grandmas' house. Clearly, that's not you!

I don't care if this is a McDonalds or some other fast food establishment you frequent. The girl at the window doesn't want to see your Shrek pajamas. So, unless you are speeding through in the middle of the night, put some clothes on. How lazy can you be? It's bad enough you go out looking like you just got up. I don't want to see you in your Shrek Pajamas or the ones with all the Minions jumping up and down, when I go to the Supermarket.

There is nothing remotely attractive about that look on you, especially when you couple it with the prison tats and plate like plugs in your ears. Check it out! It looks like some Halloween costume gone bad. Even the most down market coffee shops and convenience stores have signs that say "No Shirt, No Shoes, No Service." Clearly they didn't realize they needed to add "No Pajamas" to that sign. Save the humorous pajamas for your partner at home, and try looking into a full length mirror before venturing out next time. The Shrek look on anyone over 12 isn't a good one.

56.

DRIVERS WHO CREATE GRIDLOCK

DRIVING

No matter how many signs are posted, you don't pay one single bit of attention to them, do you? You move in inches, not feet, as you attempt to prevent anyone from turning in between you, even though there is no place for you to go. A car turns left between you and another guy sticking out into the intersection. A big sign announces a fine for creating Gridlock.

101 Things That PISS Me Off

You look the other way. No sooner do they turn and you inch your car all the way into the intersection, just as the light turns red for you. Now you are blocking the entire intersection and no one can move in any direction. You have just singlehandedly created a colossal traffic jam. Thank you!

I have to wonder why:

- Is it because you can't read?

- Are you just a selfish idiot?

- Do you need an optometrist

- Just don't give a damn?

Your choice! In the meantime the cars that had a green light are now stuck in the red again and there you sit. I want to jump out of my car and pummel you with a bag of marshmallows.

Cars are honking, but do you care? No, you are fixing your hair, texting your boyfriend or putting on lipstick. I already know who you are, so don't bother picking. You are a selfish, blind and brainless, idiot.

57.
DRIVERS WHO TURN IN FRONT OF YOU WHEN THERE IS NO ONE BEHIND YOU.

DRIVING

Who the hell taught you how to drive? Did you get your license out of a Cracker Jack box or what? I am driving the speed limit which is 50 on a two lane highway. There is no one behind me, there is no one coming in the other direction either. But there you are, the nose of your car is sticking out of that little side road and suddenly you pull out right in front of me. I slam on my brakes and hit my horn. You are oblivious and just continue pulling out, without even looking in my direction. Are you blind? Are you deaf or both?

I hit my brakes so hard that I send the dog flying from the back seat into the front, and leave 15 feet of tire rubber behind me. I nearly hit you. You continue your turn. You almost caused a major accident, but do you care? Not one bit. You step on the gas and surge from zero to ten mph limping along in front of me, like you were on vacation in Palm Springs.

One of these days that person you cut off is going to slam into your sorry ass, and you will be splattered all over the road. A road crew will then scrape your body up, put you in a plastic ziplock bag and take you to the morgue. **Bully for you!**

58.

JAYWALKERS IN THE MIDDLE OF THE STREET

THE RUDE

You must have a death wish! Can't you see me in my 5000 pound SUV zipping up the street? The light is green, which means I can go. I have the right of way, but you don't. You are **NOT** in a crosswalk so you are **fair game**. You have a target on your flower covered dress.

Just in case you don't know what a crosswalk is: white lines at a corner indicating pedestrians can safely cross the street. You don't even look. You just dart across the street like some cockroach, running for cover when a light is turned on.

Now, I can understand if there is a break in traffic and you dart from one side of the street to the other, but there is no break. I now have to slam on my brakes to avoid hitting you, so you can cross the street.

A mere 50' up there is a proper crosswalk indicated with white lines going from one side of the street to the other. There is a signal there which indicates when people on foot can cross. For those of you who cannot see well, there is even a countdown with beeps.

Stop being so bloody lazy, walk to the end of the corner and cross in the proper crosswalk. True, today may not be **Open Season** on Jaywalkers and true, you probably won't get a ticket, but one never knows when suddenly the season opens up once again and you become fair game.

59.

AUTOMATED TELEMARKETING CALLS

TELEMARKETERS

I know you are Melissa from some company in Liberty, Missouri, collecting donations for people with hoof and mouth disease, but how the hell did you get my number?

Here I am minding my own business, just sitting down for a quiet evening at home and the phone rings. I answer nicely and there is a pregnant pause while your company transfers me to India. Then Melissa comes on the line asking why I have been so hard to get hold of. I tell "Melissa" I don't want what she is selling, but she isn't real, so she keeps talking. I slam the phone down and it rings again. Finally, I am told to press #9 to opt out of future calls. I press #9 and remain optimistic. That is until the evening wears on.

But then it begins again, as if I hadn't followed instructions already and told you not to call me ever again. First it's Diane asking about my health, then Janet calls, followed by Seth and finally, Mary Lou. I press #9 for each of them.

101 Things That PISS Me Off

The following day the phone rings at dinner time and it's **YOU** again. Yes, you have gotten smart and that robo-chick really sounds like a live person, at least for the first 5 seconds. I am angry and frustrated and I want someone's head on a platter.

Hear this and hear it now: I want out of your phone bank. I'm finished pressing #9. **I don't like any of you.** You can't give me anything, and I won't ever buy anything from your company. BTW your # 9 doesn't work.

Stupid, Rude People
Piss Me Off!

A Basket Full Of
Hopeless

(My Personal Favorite)

"Oh Hell, I Mean What Else Can I Call The Rude?"

"DEPLORABLES?"

60.
IMPATIENT PEOPLE WHO DON'T LET YOU GET OFF THE ELEVATOR

A BASKET FULL OF HOPELESS

This group gave me reason for pause, because I couldn't decide which category they best belonged in; the one above or just plain **RUDE**. So here we are on the elevator heading down to the main floor of the hotel. The door slides open and feet come into focus. The feet belong to people standing poised on the other side of the elevator doors. I say excuse me, but your hearing aid is clearly turned down and you continue trying to push your way **into** the elevator. This is a learned skill!

Time Out! This is **NOT** a football game and I am not going for a touchdown. I am trying to get out of the elevator. Are you stupid or blind or both? Your 200 pound "child" continues pushing his way into the elevator, knocking me from side to side, and all I am attempting to do is **get off.** Do you not understand Basic Elevator courtesy? The elevator comes to a stop, the doors open and people, like myself, get off. Then you get on...**GET IT**? You do not force your way into an elevator like a **SALMON** swimming madly upstream, nor do you knock down those trying to get off the elevator.

This is **NOT** a game of combat; it should not be a competition to show who is the strongest. I am merely attempting to get to the Gift Shop, so stand aside and wait one moment, until I can safely disembark and then you and your **200 pound "child"** can board and try to get the elevator to lift off. Please, check the elevator weight restrictions, before launching.

61.

DEATH ROW INMATES LANGUISHING IN THEIR CELLS FOR DECADES.

A BASKET FULL OF HOPELESS

What is the matter with Kansas? You murdered 3 people 22 years ago and yet there you are, hanging around reading Law books, and **pumping iron** in the prison gym. When you're not doing either, you are slamming down three squares a day, and sleeping in a real bed, with a mattress and blankets. Doubt you had either before you became a serial killer.

101 Things That PISS Me Off

Question: Why aren't you dead already? I'll tell you why. Because some Goodie Two Shoes lawyer has decided to make a name for himself and appeal your case, over and over and over again.

- Never mind that you are a scourge on society.

- Never mind that you haven't done a days' work in your miserable life.

- Never mind that you murdered 3 innocent people, this dude wants to save your body and soul.

His reason: **You found God.** When I last looked, he or she wasn't lost, so big deal! I realize you want to make something out of your life. **Good for you.** You should have thought about that before you executed three teenagers on their way to a movie.

Memo To Serial Killer: Your victims wanted a life too. I realize you have a lot of fans, and as we all know, there is a lid for every pot. I also realize you have 10 women who have sent you proposals of marriage. I have no idea why, but to them I say, **find another hobby.** In other countries, this process moves quicker. You commit a crime and three days later you are beheaded in the Town square.

101 Things That PISS Me Off

Not so long ago in our country, Death Row was meant to be the holding place for your last few days on earth and a last meal. But today, things are totally different. Now in the USA, Death Row means decades of denial and legal mumbo jumbo, structured to spare your sorry ass!

You just got married in the Prison Chapel, with a coffee and donut reception, and twenty of your closest friends. What? **You've got a wife now, imagine that!** A condemned killer with a new wife! Clearly she was the lid who couldn't find a better hobby! On top of that, **you found God.**

So, what's next? A baby shower?

62.
ALL THE "NOT GUILTY" CRIME SUSPECTS
A BASKET FULL OF HOPELESS

Where do all the guilty go? Is anyone ever guilty of a crime? I don't think so. Just watch whenever you see a criminal in court, what do they plead 99% of the time?
Not Guilty!

- They are caught with the SMOKING gun in their hands;

- Gun powder residue all over their clothing

- A handwritten note threatening to kill someone

- Blood all over their clothing;

- A million dollar insurance policy on the victim, taken out the week before;

- An eye witness.

The plea is: **Not Guilty**. This isn't Not Guilty by Reason of Insanity, this is just plain not guilty, didn't do it, wasn't there, don't know her, don't know him, not guilty. The Alibi. He was home watching TV with the girlfriend; Visiting his mother; Going door to door selling Girl Scout Cookies; At home sleeping; 1000 Miles Away in Oklahoma.

Forget about the fact that the cellphone pings say otherwise. But there you are, that special kind of lawyer who can get up there with a straight face, and defend even the guiltiest of clients. Yes, it's true, some of them are really Not Guilty. But in your heart you **KNOW** "he" is.

>   **Memo To Legal Eagle:** Since you are so certain your client is innocent why not have him or her move in with you?

63.
BUFFETS OF ANY SORT, ANYPLACE, ANY TIME, ANY FOOD.

THE RUDE

The buffet or one can call it, the Pot Luck gathering, when it's privately held. Personally, I avoid these events like the plague, because the plague is what they remind me of.

Just think whose grubby little hands were handling those potatoes before they became, **potato salad**? Little Johnnie was just out shoveling up the dog poop and now he's in the kitchen as **Mommy's little helper**. Where were those hands, but a few short minutes ago? Hmm, building a horse manure castle or giving the dog a rectal exam? You don't know, do you? Those buffet lines are rife with **shit and snot**.

The guy in front of you just sneezed in the spaghetti marinara, and wiped his nose with his sleeve. Little Eliza just used the fork off her plate, to skewer a piece of roast beef, before she dropped it back, in favor of the sliced ham. She just got over a bout of hoof and mouth disease, but did you know that? Of course you didn't, because if you did you would never touch one morsel of food that is served in a rectangular silver pan.

A little kid with an engaging smile, is standing right in front of you when he grabs a handful of cold cuts, under the watchful eye of his mother, then changes his mind and throws them back onto the plate. Who knows where "his" hands have been?

Just the thought of someone sneezing into the pasta or putting their grubby hands onto the cheese platter makes me ill. Yes, that All You Can Eat buffet means all you can pack into your body, **enticing!** But it's what you are packing into that body that concerns me. Just where is Health and Safety when you need them?

64.

TATTOOS ON THE CHESTS OF WOMEN

A BASKET FULL OF HOPELESS

Note To Impressionable Girls:

Do you really need to canonize the birthdate of your first child on your chest? Or, alternatively, your first name or your child's first name in Gothic Letters? **Are you kidding?** Your name, your kids' name? Are you so dimwitted that you will forget it or do you just like to have those 6" Gothic Letters running from shoulder to shoulder?

101 Things That PISS Me Off

I know, it gives you something to talk about. Do you have so little in your life that the birthdate of your first kid is the only thing that has any real importance? Did your mother not already canonize your first name on your birth certificate? Perhaps you don't have a full and rich life and yes, I get it. Quite possibly you do forget your name now and again so I suppose this is your way of remembering. How about this for a great idea?

- A calendar?

- A memo pad.

- Better yet, some string tied around your finger with a note reminding you that your only child was born January 17, 2014 or that your given first name is Shannon.

Just remember, when that kid isn't speaking to you years down the line, what will you say that date is?

- Your Anniversary?

- Your dog's birthday?

- The date you first got laid?

101 Things That PISS Me Off

Why not just put a Butterfly on your ankle, write your kid's birthday in a datebook and remember this: It's cheaper and easier to put it on, than to get it off.

Then, ask yourself this **question**: Is there one outfit that you own that you would like to wear every single day for the rest of life? Young, old, fat, skinny, wrinkled? I don't think so. So why did you just let someone write in indelible ink, in 6" Gothic Letters, all over the front of your chest?

Screw This Bunch Of Brainless, Pond Scum!

Telemarketers

"God Damnit! I Told You Hitting The Keyboard Wasn't A Good Idea!

Now, Leave Me The Hell Alone!"

65.
SPAM
EMAIL

Thank you for sharing, but I do not deserve 100 emails a day. **I am not a Celebrity**. I am not a Benefactor of the poor. I am not a Charitable Foundation. I am not a Politician. I am just an ordinary person who now spends far too much time deleting the missives, that you send to me every single day.

Memo To Spammers: Stop Please!

- I already received 20 Political requests for donations, just this morning, for the same Candidate. Yes, I know it's only $10.00, but that's $200.00 just today.

- I know that I am going to miss that Seminar deadline if I don't sign up right now, before the clock strikes midnight. I'll take my chances!

- I am aware that my membership in your organization has lapsed. I already knew that.

- I realize that the Warranty on the Mercedes that I sold two years ago has lapsed. I also know you are going to send me another 20 reminders on all of the above via regular mail, so please stop spamming me.

66.

BANK TELLERS WHO HANG AROUND THE WATER COOLER WHEN PEOPLE ARE QUED IN LINE

WORKPLACE

Hello, it's me and I'm here standing in line waiting for you to finish your personal conversation with one of your co-workers. This must be super important, since you haven't even looked up to see the line that is snaking around the bank. Are you blind? What the hell do you think you are there for anyway, to unlock the doors each morning? To make a mean cup of coffee? To sit on the Bank Manager's lap?
What the hell do you think I am standing here for,

101 Things That PISS Me Off

my health? Do you think the décor in your bank is so fetching that I want to stare at it for an hour? I assure you it isn't. I don't have a crush on your Bank Manager, either. Yes, he's cute for 22, but too short and not worth losing lunch at the diner for. The line is now snaking out the door and you are still laughing and chatting it up. I am not being paid to stand here.

Memo To Indolent Bank Teller:

You, on the other hand, are being paid to work here, so do it!! I don't have all day and I don't care that your boyfriend just got a job or that your new puppy peed on the living room carpet.

Furthermore, it doesn't matter to me that your sister called you a Bitch or that your best friend is dating your Ex. Right now, I think they are both totally right. It makes little difference to me that your mother left your father and took the good china, or that your second cousin got a divorce or that Facebook locked you out because you posted too many pictures of your dog. Work it out at home.

Right now this is **MY** time. So, I am tapping my feet and clutching my deposit wondering what to do? I am furious, so before I can say water cooler, I scream out loud, "Get the manager and put some more tellers here right now." Your conversation stops and you slink back to the teller window. Everyone looks around to see who screamed. I smile secretly knowing it was me. You look annoyed, but then, so am I. Too bad you are being paid to work. You are **NOT** paid to drape your half-clad body over the water cooler, so please, undrape your body and do something.

67.

SERVICE PEOPLE WHO DON'T SHOW UP ON TIME

A BASKET FULL OF HOPELESS

Tick Tock, Tick Tock. Okay, so it's now 3:00 pm and the Cable TV company was supposed to be here during a window of noon and three.

Memo To Cable Company: Where the hell are you? Your driver may be telling you he or she is on his or her way, **but that's not true**. I mean really, how the hell long does it take to go the two miles from where they supposedly are, to where I am? Two minutes? That is **IF** he didn't stop along the way for a couple of beers; a quickie with the girlfriend; or a round of golf.

101 Things That PISS Me Off

Here's the deal: I don't really care. You are not the only fish in the well and I am tired of wasting my days waiting for your Specialist to show up. I can't even call anyone to find out where he is now, can I? Oh, that is, other than a conversation with Robo voice?

That's productive isn't it? Let's do a round of voice identification. Only then will I even have a chance of finding out where your elusive driver has escaped to. I doubt you have ever called your company and had a conversation with the **mechanical bitch** that answers your phones. Okay, game on, preview! I dial your number and "she" answers. **Main Menu:** I clear my throat and she tells me she doesn't understand. I cough and she goes back to the main menu to begin all over again. FYI, her voice identification skills suck. I hang up and grab the voodoo doll and pins.

It's now 3:45 pm and I am done with you and your windows. It's time to stick some tracking devices on your driver's trucks. You will probably find that they are spending more time servicing their girlfriend than servicing your customers. I am moving my account. Sadly, then you will spend thousands of dollars trying to lure me back into the fold with countless promises via mail. If only you spent half of that doing your job. Now wouldn't that be nice?

68.

CELLPHONES THAT TAKE PICTURES BUT DON'T GIVE YOU PHONE SERVICE.

TECHNOLOGY

Hello, hello, can you hear me now? I'm moving closer to the back door. How about now? Okay, I am moving outside, so can you hear me now?

Apple and Nokia and the rest of you Giants of Industry, I have a bitch. Why the hell is it that I can take pictures, shoot perfect videos, play a game with someone in Katmandu, but have to walk around in a circle outside, asking if the girl in my office can hear me now? Why can my phone be used to direct me to a cemetery in Timbuktu or a Museum in DC to find some insane creatures to capture, but won't "capture" a clear signal for my phone calls? This little device has grown into a regular arcade of useless trivia, but cannot replace the lamest of land lines. There are apps to test the meat on my BBQ; arrange some instant sexual encounter; blow out birthday candles; annoy someone with screeching sounds or receive a fake call to remove me from an irritating situation.

101 Things That PISS Me Off

There are even apps that will tell you where you pooped last or the best place to pee. **Really?** I have a cellphone in order to make calls, so what about that don't you get? I love that I can take pictures of my dog and Selfies of me walking into walls, but why the **HELL** can't I make a call where I don't have to say, "Can you hear me now?"

It's really nice that my phone lets me:

- Video the escapades of others,

- Play mindless, unimportant games,

- Waste time trolling the internet

- Post inappropriate pictures.

- Provides an app of a person staring at me all day,

- Counts sheep to help me sleep,

- Sends inappropriate texts

- Unearths all the witches in my neighborhood;

But, does NOT give me a clear signal to make or get a phone call. **WHAT**!!!!

I am totally sick of dropped calls and saying "Can you hear me now?" **"Can you hear me now?"** So, massive Giant Corporations, what is your solution to this major problem?

You increase the size of the phone to make it give the customer:

- Better quality videos;

- Be able to send a message to a tribal person in the Kalahari;

- Turn our house alarm on from 100 miles away;

- Turn our car on from inside the house;

- Turn the heat or lights on when we forget.

- Probably even spray for pests!

Great! **Good for you!** I'll be damned. I am going back to the old fashioned way, the flip phone, so that I can make a proper, clear, uninterrupted phone call.

So screw you.

You Bet Your Freaking Life, I'm Still Pissed Off!

How About Email?

"Will You Please STOP Already? I Have A Splitting Headache."

69.
SMOKERS WHO HOLD THEIR CIGARETTES AWAY FROM THEIR TABLES SO AS NOT TO OFFEND THEIR GUESTS

SMOKERS

What the hell are you doing? I'm choking! Clouds of nicotine infested smoke are **drifting** from your table over to mine. Yes, we are in a bar. I get it. But why don't you have that cigarette in an ashtray on your table? I know how much you love your Aunt Fanny and Uncle Roger. I get that they don't smoke and you do.

I appreciate your consideration, holding your smoldering cancer stick away from the table so you don't offend them. **Nice work**. But guess what? I am not your Aunt Fanny, but I don't smoke either and frankly I don't care about you or your relatives. Keep your damned cigarette smoke at your own table or I will come over there and pour a pitcher of water on it and you.

70.
STRIP SEARCHES IN AIRPORTS
WORKPLACE

I don't know why I even bother to get dressed before flying out somewhere. From now on, I am arriving at the airport in pajamas, because I end up taking everything off anyway. I then have to place my entire wardrobe into tiny plastic containers and pile my computer on top. I still set the alarm off. I have a card for my knee, but you don't care.

Now I have to stand in what little clothing I have left in a machine where someone can see through what I'm wearing. This is the job for a pervert! I'm in a machine, naked and not even having a good time.

But that isn't even the final humiliation. No matter how little I have on, or how clinging it is, you seem to think I could get something between me and my "Calvins." I can't get a note paper underneath my skin tight tee shirt, but you still want to pat me down which is "code" **for feeling me up. Security!**

There she is, looking like the head guard in a maximum security prison. I try to point out the **ONLY** thing in my shirt are my **boobs** and all that is in my skin tight leggings, are my legs, but **SHE** continues "patting" me down like some criminal. Finally, I am released with just my watch as the villain.

As a final humiliation, in the rush to get dressed and catch my flight, I leave my boarding pass and cellphone in one of the six plastic containers. I race back to the TSA Security, identify myself, grab my belongings and rush back to the Gate just in time to see the doors shutting.

Thanks for the memories!

71.

MAGAZINE SUBSCRIPTIONS THAT NEVER ARRIVE

SNAIL MAIL

You are really on the ball when it comes to luring me with promises of $1.00 magazines. Those babies just keep on coming, but not every month. I have a stack of your free and practically free offers, cards and letters. Then there are those gifts you say I just won and I have fallen for that one every time.

101 Things That PISS Me Off

But after a month of your magazine Love Fest I ask, Where the hell is my copy of **Vanity Fair**? What about Time and Newsweek? Were the covers so great that the Postman decided to read them first? Did you send them to someone else? You sold me, you charged me and I want my magazines looking vibrant and new today, not dog-eared and rifled through the following month.

You promised, so get your head out of the latest issue of the **National Enquirer** and find my copies of Vanity Fair, Time and Newsweek, or are you still reading them?

Then, just when I have had enough, you charge my card for the following year, and it's a whopping $58.00 for one magazine. I call to cancel, **you swing into overdrive** and Holly Go Lightly offers me the super-duper special, only for me, $2.00! I have won the bet your life prize. How can I resist, but I do!

Even when I say **NO** to that offer, you have more up your sleeves. Finally, I have no recourse but to say yes to **$2.00 for 6 months.. including Vanity Fair!** Here is my suggestion: How about you make sure I get the magazines I wanted and paid for, first time around? I don't really care how you accomplish this task. Just do it!

72.

PARENTS WHO BRING CHILDREN WITH THEIR TOYS TO A NICE RESTAURANT.

THE RUDE

It's finally here, after a grueling week at work, Saturday. My husband and I have planned a lovely dinner at a romantic restaurant by the lake. No sooner are we seated and it starts. I hear a **whirring noise** that disrupts our quiet evening. It sounds like a helicopter. What IS that noise?

OMG it's a life sized version of R2D2 complete with raucous sound. I glance over to the next table and see that it is littered with toys, and being overseen by a two year old.

What is up with this? Is that really a toddler with an IPad? It can't be! There's another one playing on what I can only assume is your IPhone! It's an IPhone 6, in the mitts of a 4 year old. Are you kidding? They are now banging on the table with the silverware and one of the adults is showing them how to make the loudest possible noise using a tablespoon and a glass, while the others smile and wave. Is this the new reality?

101 Things That PISS Me Off

Am I asking too much to think that I can go out to dinner with my husband or with friends and not have the restaurant look like a version of Chucky Cheese on steroids?

Toys belong at home, **not** in a restaurant. Are your children so badly behaved that you must bribe them? A small missive arrives on my table and **lands in my soup**. It is a Lego. You get up and come to retrieve it, smiling, hand extended.. I want to shake some sense into you, but I refrain, sensing danger from your side of the room. You laugh and try to make it seem like this is normal behavior, "**they are just kids**" you joke.

Well, if they were my kids they would either behave or be home. Let them have their Star Wars figures and their Minions on the floor of your very own living room, **NOT** on the floor of this restaurant or take your dog and pony show to McDonalds. They have a play area just for this sort of thing. In the meantime, I can't help but notice you and your friends are laughing and chatting, and have all but ignored your kids as they wreak havoc on everyone else. **Nice Work!**

73.

PARENTS WHO BRING SMALL CHILDREN TO GALAS ON NEW YEARS EVE.

THE RUDE

So what have we here? It's New Years Eve and we are at the luxurious 4 Seasons Hotel, **$700 a couple** without accommodations. Suddenly the flow of champagne and sounds of flute music are interrupted by the wails of a child, crying.

I look around in horror to see a 6 month old being danced around the floor by an elderly woman. A few feet away is another table and a screaming 3 year old whose father has chosen her as his unwilling dance partner. She is not a happy camper. The baby and the toddler are now screaming in unison, and not with delight. What the hell are you doing? This is an infant and toddler who should be in bed? It's after midnight!

Why are your small children celebrating New Year's Eve with us?

One child isn't even old enough to sit in a chair and has never even lived long enough to see a New Years Eve. Why then have you chosen to drag him along to this expensive Gala at a Luxury Hotel?

101 Things That PISS Me Off

Did you misread the hotel's name? It does say Four Seasons right on the front of that huge sign. It should not be mistaken for the 4 Seasons Child Care Center which is around the corner. This is the luxurious Four Seasons Hotel where dinner and dancing set a couple back nearly $700.00. No accommodations. But there you all are, baby in tow in one family, a toddler in tow in another.

It's midnight and you and your companion are now dancing, squashing the infant between you.. He continues to scream, but you pay no attention as you laugh and carry on. In any other place, this would be considered abuse. That kid is 6 months old and should be home sleeping, but you two have decided to share the joy, whatever that means to a 6 month old and the rest of us.

Finally after nearly 3 hours of relentless fussing and crying, you decide to remove the baby and place him where he or she should have been all evening, in your hotel room, with a mother, father, grandmother, grandfather, aunt, uncle or a baby sitter. The toddler is still screaming and dad, well, you are still dancing her around the room gleefully.

Memo To Dad: Give us all a break. Not our kid, not our problem. Call the concierge and get a baby sitter. It's New Years Eve!

Pissed Off Yet? Dude, I'm Just Getting Started!

Snail Mail

"Yes, Life Is A BITCH! But, I've Got NO ONE To Complain To!"

74.

IGNORANT PEOPLE WHO RALLY BEHIND ISSUES THEY DON'T UNDERSTAND

A BASKET FULL OF HOPELESS

OMG, what is wrong with our Country anyway? There are requirements for someone:

- **to get a drivers' license**

- **a real estate license**

- **to teach a class**

- **have a child care facility**

- **to fly a plane**

- **become a hairdresser**

- **own a dog**

You need to get educated and then take a test. But you don't' need to pass a test to vote and advocate for or against things you don't understand at all.

101 Things That PISS Me Off

Listen up, dude! You are currently on welfare, but you're voting for someone who wants to take it away. Does that make sense? You get food stamps, but you're voting for a guy who wants to abolish that program. Really? You think the world is coming to an end and have amassed an arsenal of weapons in your basement. But that "end of the world" date has come and gone and we are all still here. Don't believe me? Pinch yourself! But what do you do? You just move the "**end of the world** date" ahead!

Are you insane or just uneducated? You have imaginary monsters coming out at night from under your bed and think the government is out to get you. I know you need an arsenal to protect yourself, but you are more worried about keeping your guns, than your food stamps. You want to end abortion, but you don't care that kids are being abused every day. You preach family values, then have an affair with your neighbors' wife. Wake up and smell the coffee dude. You need to get some education under that oversized belt of yours. Understand what you are fighting for and against before you open your chops and start mouthing off.

75.

PEOPLE WHO CALL AND DON'T SAY ANYTHING AT ALL.

TELEMARKETERS

Who the hell are you anyway? I have just settled in for dinner and the phone rings. I reluctantly rise from the couch and make my way into the breakfast room where the phone resides. In my best voice I greet the caller, who has just disrupted my dinner. "Good Evening." Silence followed by some annoying sounds. "Hello, Hello?" I repeat again into the phone. More annoying tiny sounds, but no person is attached to the sounds.

Who the devil are you and what do you want? I get that "silence is golden" but **YOU** called me. Somehow in your silence, I already know you are some annoying telemarketer. You clearly have heard the tone of my voice and decided you had best not say anything. So all I hear are giggles, very professional. I hang up on you and I silently dare you to call again. If you do I will read you the riot act and rain all over your telemarketing parade. Do not call and disrupt my day or my dinner and then say nothing. Have the courage of your convictions and at least announce who you are so I can hang up on you then.

76.
PEOPLE WHO KNOW EVERYTHING

A BASKET FULL OF HOPELESS

We all have them in our lives, don't we? The Brother, Sister, Son, Daughter, Son-In-Law, Daughter-In-Law, friend, the newspaper guy at the corner. They come in all shapes and sizes, don't they? Tall, short, young, old, fat, skinny, but they have one thing in common. **They know everything.** Not just some things, everything. You cannot tell these people anything, because they already know it all!

That's why their lives are usually working so well, **NOT**! That is why they are living in a rented room or a double wide trailer. That is why they just lost their fully paid for condo. That is why they can't find a job. That is why they start believing their own stories. I mean why should they listen to you? Why should they take your advice? Why should they pay attention to any professional at all?

101 Things That PISS Me Off

They wrote the book on everything, just ask them about:

- Financing A House

- Gardening

- Building A Shed Or Anything Structural

- Raising Kids

- Repairing Your Car

- Writing A Book

- Starting A Business

- Raising Bees

- Doing Hair

- Losing Weight

- Buying Stocks

- Fixing Your Relatonship

101 Things That PISS Me Off

They are experts in every field, except when it comes to knowing anything. They listen to no one and end up with their life in shambles.

A closer look at these "know it alls" and you can see they have:

- Been Divorced Multiple Times

- Work In A Dead End Job

- Have Out Of Control Kids

- Never Written Anything In Their Life

- Are Overweight

- Living In A Rented Apartment

So clearly, they shouldn't be advising anyone.

Memo To Know It Alls:

It's probably a good idea for you to stop acting like you know everything and start listening to other people for a change. I say that because frankly, your life is a mess. You need some serious help dude, so why are you dispensing advice when you don't take it yourself? Pathetic but true. Seriously, don't you think there might be areas of your life that could use some improvement? Try listening instead of dispensing, for a change, it might help.

77.

REALITY SHOWS WITH HILLBILLIES; BEARDS OR KIDS IN SCANTY COSTUMES.

A BASKET FULL OF HOPELESS

Personally, I am up to here with tots in full make-up, sequins and faux heels. Give me a break! That child is 3 and you already have her **tarted up** in a strapless sequin number, with enough makeup on to cover the Victoria's Secret Models' faces for an entire year. What is up with that? Between the toddler pageants and the fly away beards we are a country in chaos.

I know you want to live your life vicariously through your child, but using her as a canvas for face paint is downright bizarre. Use yourself! There is nothing funny about a tiny tot strutting her stuff up a runway in a strapless dress. While we are at it, what makes television production companies think that looking at someone whose beard resembles an overcrowded birds nest is attractive? I don't know.

Don't viewers get that these **Reality Characters** head into full makeup before shooting their show and that they don't actually **live** in a log cabin? It's a television show folks. They live in mansions, fly helicopters and have the millions of dollars they have made fooling you.

So what's up with you? That pioneer look is not a good one, especially this century. Your day is over, finished, **finito**, done. You are not someone living off the land in a log cabin, without access to a razor. Yes, unique concept the **RAZOR**. It is meant to take hair off of your face.

However, should you choose to have a beard, the razor also helps with that too. You can trim that beard and make it look tidy. Right now you look like Grizzly Adams on steroids. Like someone who has been shipwrecked on an island for a year. This is **NOT** a good look. You are a mess! It may be a trend, but you can recover. Just trim that overgrown, unkempt bush.

78.

REALITY SHOWS IN GENERAL... ENOUGH ALREADY!

A BASKET FULL OF HOPELESS

Spoiler Alert: These are television shows **FOLKS** and they are scripted. Get that through your heads. Those people that are "stranded" on an island, naked and afraid, are **NOT** alone. If you think they are, perhaps it's time to get back on your meds or to seek professional help. Someone is out there folks, shooting the film, making sure no one dies or falls off a cliff or gets ill from eating a poison frog. So relax and don't fret. Those stranded folks will all get back to dry land in due time, bug bites, stories and all.

The Production companies are always looking for a way to reel you in and they continue testing the waters.

They are not real, but the reality is, **enough already.** They have overstepped the boundaries of good taste too many times.

79.

WARNINGS AT THE END OF DRUG COMMERCIALS

WORKPLACE

Hey, listen up Drug Companies. Have you ever bothered to tune in to your own commercials? The fine print part I mean. I doubt it. They have been structured by huge PR Firms and Legal eagles to reel people in before dropping the disclosure into their laps First they are lulled into a sense of calm and hope. A little cartoon peers out at them from a sidewalk offering some life saving pills. .

So, you need a medication for depression or fatigue or chronic irritated whatever, and that new medication sure sounds great, doesn't it? The very best thing you can do is **NOT** listen to the warning at the end, that quietly describes what can happen if you take this drug. You can die, get a blood clot, have a stroke, a heart attack. If you live, you could be disabled. Don't take while pregnant, nursing, taking other drugs, over 30, over 40, if still breathing, or if you have symptoms of any of the above.

101 Things That PISS Me Off

Wow, I have arthritis in my hand, so you can cure that but kill me in the process? **IF** anyone stays tuned for the disclaimers at the end of your flowery commercials, they would have to be nuts to pop a pill. At first, you watch mesmerized, as funny faced cartoons pop out of sidewalks singing the benefits of an anti-depression medication, while happy people run in the grass flying kites or playing ball, because they have taken one of your super-duper, special pills.

Then, there it is, that disclaimer hidden at the very end and it pops that bubble of happiness. Or it should. Tiny print appears and rapidly disappears. Then a soft, but stern voice warns you about the hazards of this very same medication. You are using an assault weapon to kill a mosquito. Your drug could kill me, so hey, Giant Phamaceutical Company, how about this for a suggestion? Why not fix the drugs so they don't kill you, cripple you, maim you, or otherwise ruin your life, or take them off the market?

80.

LACK OF ROOM TO MOVE IN COACH CLASS

WORKPLACE

Urgent Memo To Airlines: Okay, I get that you have taken the fun out of flying, but really, does flying need to be torture? I'm freezing! The guy in front has lowered his seat an inch and barricaded me in, preventing me from going to the midget-sized bathroom. I'm a prisoner in seat 32 C unable to even reach around and ask him to put his seat up. I try in vain to recline my seat, it moves an inch. You are now occupying the aisle, offering to sell me a bag of chips and a glass of soda water, $6.00! I paid to be tortured.

I am not a midget, I am not a child, I am an adult. I don't ask for much. Here are my requests in a nutshell:

- Take off and land safely

- Get me where I am going in one piece

- Allow me to get up and pee without using a can opener to get out of my seat

101 Things That PISS Me Off

- Feed me something I can identify

- Give me a seat that reclines more than an inch

- Turn the freezing air conditioning down or give blankets in Coach

Isn't it enough that I have to bring my own lunch? Isn't it enough that I have to pay to check my bags? Isn't it enough that I have to get undressed to get through security to board your aircraft? I would think that you would have some mercy, some kindness and allow me to sit, slightly reclined, in your bench type seats during that 6 hour flight and let me arrive without icicles on my face.

How much can a person take? The stewardesses who used to say "fly me" are no longer around or have been replaced by older, less sleek models. I already had to undress and put my stuff in a plastic box; was seen naked in a body scan; had a fat woman feel me up and waited in single file to march down the boarding ramp, get onto your aircraft and use a shoehorn to get into my seat.

Have some sympathy and at least give me a bit of elbow room and a way to go to the bathroom. I know you have to make money, but the man in front of me is currently sprawled out in my lap.

81.
RELIGIOUS ZEALOTS OF ANY SIZE SHAPE AND RELIGION

A BASKET FULL OF HOPELESS

I see you, stomping around, pounding and screaming homophobic slurs, while thrashing about with a snake or some other serpent. You self-righteous **SOB's** are usually the ones who have the most skeletons in their closet. You, with the Praise the Lord, **BUT** pass the ammunition mentality, sending people of all shapes and sizes to hell with a lash of the tongue, and your hand selected words from God.

I ask you: just what are the family values of a guy who preaches hell-fire and damnation, but is screwing his neighbors' wife? Where are the values of the guy who shrieks to all within earshot that gay people are going to hell, yet sits at his computer each night looking at gay porn? I tell you what that is: **Hypocrisy**, and I am sick to death of it. You want family values?

Try practicing it!. Don't run your mouth about Heaven and Hell, then go home and slap your wife around. Don't preach about the word of God, and abuse your kids. Walk the walk or shut the hell up. I am sick and tired of people who sin all week long, then go to church on Sunday and wash it all away with a few Hail Mary's. While you're at it, stop saying, that the **devil made you do it**. Stop thinking you can just "find" God and make it all better, just because you say so. Stop trying to **"find"** God, because he isn't lost.

82.

PEOPLE WHO WANT TO FORCE FEED THEIR BELIEFS ON EVERYONE

THE RUDE

I know you are a prophet of God and that he speaks through you. That's nice, I'm happy for you. While we are on the subject, I have a bridge to sell you in downtown Palm Springs and I would rather you not waste your time inundating me with your crazy talk.

I have my views, you have yours. I don't like your views, but I say, okay, have them. Just don't try to torment me into accepting them, otherwise I just might have to sell you that bridge.

This is America and we are free to make choices, even though, I think yours are off the radar, I respect the fact that you think **God** speaks to you and tells you not to drink the water and that the end of the World is coming on January 1, 2017.

I know you have the task of convincing people that you **ARE** the voice of God, if you want to continue being a prophet. I appreciate your unrelenting passion for the subject.

Just know that I do **not** think you were sent by God to help us out of certain damnation. God has better taste. I am perfectly willing to take my chances with both Heaven and Hell. Thank you very much, but I don't need your help or your advice. I respect your views, just keep them to yourself, please. Good luck with your work, both God and I wish you the very best.

83.

LEMONS: ANY PRODUCT THAT DOESN'T WORK

JUNK

I waited 3 weeks and was wildly excited to get that new product that I ordered from China. I open it up, stick in the batteries and, oops, it doesn't work. Now what? Then, a week later the tee shirts I ordered in Small arrived, marked Medium, but I couldn't get them over one shoulder. Now what? I ordered some prescription drugs on the Internet and they arrived from India, but they are the wrong prescription. Now what?

I'll tell you what, I'm stuck with lemons and I can't even make lemonade. So what do I do now? Let me see! I could call you and probably end up in India or Thailand, Mexico or the Philippines, with someone who, while sympathetic, is unable or unwilling to help. I request a Supervisor and they put me on hold listening to annoying pre-recorded screeching music. They offer to send me a return sticker or a credit or to replace the faulty item.

101 Things That PISS Me Off

I accept the latter and wait 3 more agonizing weeks for my package. It arrives and it's the very same prescription; the exact extra small tee shirts marked Medium that fit over one shoulder; or the product that doesn't work.

I call again and **you** answer, but this time you are in Costa Rica. I spell out my problem, syllable by syllable, and you make the same offers, return, credit, replacement. This time I accept the credit and vow never to buy any more lemons from China. That is until the next time something catches my fancy.

Message To Self: Buy products Made in USA!

Message to China: How about checking stuff out for fit and to see if it works, **before** you ship?

84.
LACK OF QUALITY CONTROL IN MERCHANDISE.

JUNK

Why do I have to repair your faulty products? Is it so difficult to make it right in the first place? I just brought this jacket home and the buttons fell off when I tried it on. I put that brand new necklace on and it fell apart. I am not a jewelry repair operation or a seamstress. That's your department. What about that don't you understand? You manufacture clothing. Make sure the buttons are sewn on right so that I don't end up with them in my hand. In case you don't know, they belong on the clothing. I am on my way out, now what? I don't even have a needle or thread and can't find a safety pin.

The buttons in question hold this dress together in the front, so what the hell am I supposed to do now? Chewing gum? Scotch tape? **Perhaps, a paper clip.** Maybe I just need to forget this new dress and change. I hate you! Why not pay better attention to your line of products and make sure they don't fall apart on receipt.

Otherwise I might just Yelp or Tweet or Instagram and upset your little fashion empire.

85.

PEOPLE WHO HAVE EXCUSES FOR EVERYTHING

A BASKET FULL OF HOPELESS

News Flash: It isn't your Aunt Millie's fault that you don't have a job. The notion that your parents' dogs were barking and kept you up last night, didn't make you miss your interview this morning.

You didn't lose that job you wanted because your mom forgot to wake you up. You're 40 years old, living at home and not paying rent. You get up at noon, fall into the kitchen and demand that your mother make you breakfast.

Then you drag your lazy ass into the TV room, use your last bit of energy to pick up the remote control and lay back down on the couch to play video games. At 3 pm you muster up enough strength to call out to your mom to make you lunch, which she does.

You are still in your pajamas at 7pm when dinner is on the table. You amble to the table, pick up a plate, help yourself and head back to the couch. You are a lazy slob. At 10 pm you drag your body off the couch and head back to your room, which is covered with empty food wrappers and soda cans. You leave your dirty dinner plates on the floor in the TV room for your mother to pick up and wash. The following morning, the routine is varied slightly as you take a moment to complain that you missed out on an interview because the dogs kept you up all night long.

Why are you living at home anyway at the age of 40? Your pathetic excuses are pissing me off. You being dealt a raw hand by the Universe isn't the fault of some immigrant who is working in the fields picking tomatoes. You won't head to the fields to pick tomatoes will you? You aren't about to get your lazy, entitled ass out of bed at 4:00 am and dirty your lily white hands picking corn, are you? You are too good for that, right? Wrong! So listen, how about this for an idea: Stop complaining about everything and blaming everyone for your lot in life.

I rest my case. Get a job, a place to live, make your own dinner and stop complaining.

86.

PEOPLE WHO ARE NOT ON TIME

THE RUDE

Hey you, Mr. Eye Doc, Madame Hairdresser, Dr. Cavity, my time is valuable too. I don't care that you are a doctor, dentist, hairdresser, whatever. You make an appointment, guess what? I stopped what I was doing to get in the car and get to your office on time. I am there waiting for you and I don't want to be. **Nice magazines and I've read them already.**

I look at my clock and it's now 20 minutes after my appointment time. What the hell is up? I go to the receptionist and ask her. She tells me you're running late.

Really? I didn't know that! I just thought you were still out to lunch at "21." Of course, you are running late, that is why I am standing at the desk asking what is happening. How late are you, I ask? About 45 minutes is the reply.

If I were 45 minutes late for my appointment with you, I would be rescheduled, wouldn't I? But you get to be 45 minutes late for me and I must grin and bear it.

I guess that is how it works in your world, but not in mine. **Here is a suggestion** Mr. Medical Doctor; Ms. Hairdresser; Get up earlier; Gas the car up the night before; Leave enough space between appointments; Work a bit faster; Make sure your other patients, clients, whatever, are on time; and be on time yourself, I am.

Life Without Being Pissed Off, Just Isn't Life!

Junk

"At Least It's Got A Roof and Indoor Lighting!"

87.

PRISONERS WHO PROFIT FROM ILLICIT OR BAD DEEDS

CRIMINALS

MEMO TO MURDERER: You are an unrepentant murderer, in jail for a ghastly crime. You are not an esteemed Member of the local Country Club. You already have more privileges than any homeless person around, but why should you? Now, you want to write a book about your life? Who the hell cares? I know you want everyone to understand that your mother was an abusive alcoholic, who locked you in the basement and fed you a diet of dead mice. Your lawyer already told the court you were shuttled around the foster system and never knew good old dad. **OMG**, my 82 year old neighbor has a far worse story than that. Frankly Convict 13578, no one cares that you were bullied, so was I. **Big deal**! Grow some balls! The difference is, you killed a bunch of strangers, just because you had it rough as a kid.

   Flash: You don't get to profit off of your crime dude. You get to stay exactly where you are, locked up and away from civilized society.

Write your memoir, if you must, but keep it to yourself, your fans and your cellmate. If you want to do something meaningful, spend time thinking about why you did what you did and how you can make your life have some meaning. Until then, take up needlepoint. Make a quilt or learn to bake a great banana bread.

88.

RUDE PEOPLE...

RUDE

Where were you brought up, in a barn? How hard can it be? You should be teaching your children some manners, so perhaps you can learn some right along with them. Two little words that mean so much, excuse me! Now I realize that for a lot of you that is quite difficult, because you were never taught any manners at all.

101 Things That PISS Me Off

That's why you think it's perfectly okay:

- To eat food with your hands

- Wear a hat in a restaurant

- Fart in public

- Belch at the dinner table

- Butt in line

- Use your sleeve as a napkin

- Wear pajamas out in public

- Suck food from your fingers at the dinner table

- Walk in front of someone and knock them over

- Never open a car door for a lady

- Curse like a sailor and

- Dress like a homeless person

Dr. Hannibal Lechter had a really good idea. **He ate the rude!** You are precisely the sort of person the good Doctor enjoyed sautéing with a fine white wine or skewering with some mushrooms and peppers. So here's a novel suggestion for all rude people to avoid getting eaten or worse: When you walk in front of someone, cut someone off while heading into a building, let the door slam in their face, accidentally, or bang into them…say **excuse me**.

89.

PEOPLE WHO MAKE AN APPOINTMENT TO DELIVER A SERVICE OR PRODUCT AND DON'T SHOW UP OR CALL CUSTOMER SERVICE

So where the hell is my firewood at $250.00 a cord? It's freezing outside and I am down to my last few pieces of wood.

I called you three weeks ago and you quoted a price to me. Did the price increase since then? Was it something I said? Are you angry, sad, upset, rageful? Did you lose my address, my phone number, my name? If your answer is no to all of these then I must just believe that you are a crappy businessman. No wonder you live in a hovel surrounded by wood chips. No wonder you have to live with your mother, sister, brother, aunt.

There truly is a very special place in hell for you. You sound normal, but you aren't. Business must be booming, but it's not. How do I know that? Because you didn't call or show up when you said you would. That date is called an appointment. If you can't come you call and cancel.

That is what grown up business people do. You are a slacker. You don't deserve to be running the family store. So hang up your saw and hand back your drivers' license, that is if you have one, and go to work slinging burgers at Big Mac, if they will have you. I'm going out to chop down the barn.

90.

THE NEVER ENDING ROADWORKS PROJECT

A BASKET FULL OF HOPELESS

I am sick to death of driving through, around and over, old, unfinished Road Works Ghost projects. There they are, the signs that say **Road Works** and the threats to double your fines in those "construction" areas.

There are the telltale tractors and dying cement mixers; the orange "witch's hats" and tape indicating work, but where the hell are the workers? **It's like a ghost site.** Are they out to lunch? Having a beer or two at their local pub? Taking a snooze?

Flash: I know where they aren't! They aren't working. The trucks sit, empty and idle; The cement mixer is covered in cobwebs and hasn't seen the light of day in a month; No doubt, the cement is hardened inside! The sectioned road is barren; Nothing has changed in months, except for the inconvenience of not having two lanes in either direction. That has been the same story since March 1, 2015. I want this job, if you can call it that. Imagine this: getting paid for **NOT** working.

101 Things That PISS Me Off

So now, I am being detoured over and around a section of the highway that has been **"under construction"** for the past 6 months. But no one is there, so no wonder it's taking so long. But wait: I see signs of life in front of me.

There they are, **the workers.** They have moved to a new section of road and are now blocking that off into one lane, so they can trim a tree and fill a pothole. What the hell is going on? What about the huge mess you left 3 miles back? Turn your truck around, and **get the hell back** there and finish what you started last March. How's that for an idea whose time has come? Finish what you start, before you go making a mess someplace else!

91.

PEOPLE WHO DON'T CLEAN UP AFTER THEIR DOGS

THE RUDE

Hey you! Don't pretend you don't see me! You, the one with the dog that resembles a small horse. Your dog just took a dump on my front lawn. If you think that I didn't see him lay that huge pile of crap just now, you are wrong! Now, I get that you need a small truck to move his waste, but that's your problem.

To make matters worse, I don't see a shovel or a garbage bag or even some paper towels in your hand, which means, you intended to leave this pile of crap to compost on my lawn. Well, that's not happening.

I just took a picture of you and your horse with my Smartphone, and I intend to send it to every social media outlet in the world, along with your name, address and phone number. That should embarrass your ass.

If you don't wish to be an instant Internet sensation, then here is what you need to do right now: Get some trash bags and shovel up that crap, before someone slips and falls into it. Consider this, invest in a pooper scooper and pick up that shit before someone like me gets really angry and shoves you, face first, into it.

UGLY!

More Shit Hits The Fan... The Bitch Is Back!

Corporate Greed

"What's A Little Payoff Among Friends? My Lips Are Sealed! Two Words: Off Shore!"

92.
HIGH PRESCRIPTION DRUG PRICES
CORPORATE GREED

This is America and I'm totally confused. My father is 83 and can barely walk, but he has to drive 1500 miles, passport in hand, through a Border Control station and into Canada to buy his medications! But there you are, the giant Pharmaceuticals, dotting the landscape in Mississippi, a stone's throw from his house. I can't help but ask **WHY?** Yes, why can't he get his medications closer to his home. **Drug Lords** have jacked the price of those medications up so high, he cannot afford to buy them. You claim it's because of the R & D, but I think it's because of the **AMD!** That Almighty Dollar!

I realize you Giants of Industry are in the business of making money, but how much is enough and when does it end? Yes, there is the costly Research and Development, trying out these high tech drugs on rabbits, chickens, mice and the homeless, but surely that gets amortized at some point?

Just recently, you raised the price of a drug by 15,000 percent! Are you kidding? But maybe, the joke's on you. Hoardes of prescription drug hostages are now making their way across the border to our friends in Canada or buying that very same prescription online at a fraction of the price. **That equates to Lost Sales!** You are nothing but Drug Lords in Lab Coats.

Memo To Drug Lords: It's a dangerous world out there and someone or something could just come and move onto your turf, so why not mix some compassion in with the greed.

93.

CORPORATE GREED

A BASKET FULL OF HOPELESS

News Flash: I don't have access to a Corporate Jet or even First Class on the airplane. I can't write off my Toyota as an expense or that $500 sushi dinner or even a Big Mac. I don't have an Offshore Bank Account to **"hide"** my assets, because there are **NO** assets to hide.

But you, the 1%ers hide it all.

You take everything and give back nothing. The real bitch about this, is that even though you take so much, you still want to deprive the rest of us of our Social Security, Medicare, Health Care, or any other type of hand up, not out, that might be needed. **Get it straight:** People pay into Social Security and Medicare with every dollar that they slave to earn, yet you call those **"entitlement"** programs. Really?

Since when is the Social Security that I paid into for 40 years entitlement? Well, I guess if you look at it that way, **YES**, I am *entitled* to get the money that I paid into that program and worked so hard for. I am "entitled" to it! So here's a suggestion: You can take your 1 % super rich mentality and put it where the sun does shine, on an island in one of your off-shore accounts. While you're at it, keep your grubby mitts off my Social Security and Medicare.

94.

CREDIT CARD COMPANIES THAT DON'T LOWER THEIR INTEREST RATES

CORPORATE GREED

I am trying to wrap my head around this mathematical problem. My mortgage is under 4.00%. My bank is paying me an interest rate on my savings that is less than 1%!

My mailbox is **overflowing** with offers for 0% interest for the next 15 months to pay off bills. I accept. Thank you all very much. Then, **the fine print**, which requires a magnifying glass. There it is! At the end of the 15 months, you are going to charge me 20% for any unpaid balance.

If I buy something, during that time and use the card, the interest rate is 27%. Are you kidding? The bank isn't even giving me enough interest on my savings to buy a Starbucks coffee next month, yet you are charging me nearly 27%! What the hell is going on? I don't want to buy your bank, nor do I want to fund your next acquisition. I 'm okay paying a fair and equitable rate on my card, but this is robbery in small print.

That sort of interest used to be called usury and was illegal. Maybe it still is and you, the Robber Barons of Banking, have just found a clever way around it.

95.

LACK OF FULL DISCLOSURE BY PHARMECEUTICAL GIANTS

CORPORATE GREED

It's great to be you, isn't it? Sitting at the pinnacle of an industry that most everyone needs at one time or another. An alarming number of people **need** to have your products, because you have worked your magic and made sure they take something for everything, no matter how small it is.

- Headaches

- Depression

- Toothache

101 Things That PISS Me Off

- Pains
- Arthritis
- Sore foot
- Sore toe
- Cuts
- Abrasions
- Nose Bleed
- Runny Nose
- Dry Eyes
- Sleeplessness
- Skinned Knee

You name it, and you have a pill for it and if you don't, you will make one up! Actually, come to think of it, I think I should call this Lack of Any Disclosure!

101 Things That PISS Me Off

One fine day, in the presence of your legal team, you should read the Full Disclosure at the very end of your Television ads. You will need a magnifying glass and pause button, so you can try to decipher the very small print.

Pause, as the voice-over rushes through the various maladies that can befall you, should you decide to believe the little animation, who just popped out of the sidewalk. That cute character, wants to help you with your depression, anxiety, blood pressure, cholesterol, fatigue, migraines. He is there to make your life better with a little pill! But, **wait for it**, you could have a stroke, heart attack, blood clot, seizure or just up and die. True, it is hard to comprehend the hasty messages at the end of all of the drug ads.

Put away the beer and popcorn, turn the sound up to full volume and pay attention. Yes, that little voice just said you could die. Ask yourself, do I really want to be taking that? Isn't there another, better, safer way to deal with my headache, anxiety, depression, joint pain? The answer might just be **YES.** OMG, there they are again with that fine print, at the end of another flashy, happy family drug commercial.

People are singing and dancing, playing games or just working out, smiling. But not you, because you are not taking **THAT** medication and according to "them," you should be. But hold on and listen, you could die or have a stroke or heart attack or suffer loss of vision, loss of hearing. Serious stuff, hidden under a cartoon. So, forget about that slap-happy cartoon and listen carefully for the end. It's worth it!

96.

MOVING COMPANIES THAT REFUSE TO TAKE RESPONSIBILITY FOR BREAKAGE

A BASKET FULL OF HOPELESS

I don't know, how difficult can it be to wrap items up, pack them carefully in a carton, move them onto a truck and have them arrive in the same condition as they left my home in? That hand-painted vase lasted for 125 years moving to three countries, until you got your grubby mitts on it. That hand painted vase once belonged to my Great Grandmother and was in one piece when you packed it.

You drove 1000 miles and were not involved in any motor vehicle incidents along the way. Your truck didn't encounter a sinkhole! You took the carton out of the truck and carried it in a single piece into my new home. However, when I unpacked it, the vase was in twenty pieces, but you say, **"not our responsibility."**

So I ask you, whose responsibility is it? The postman, the traffic cop, my neighbor, the Manager at my building? I don't get it. I didn't drive it 1000 miles from New York to Florida. **You did**. I didn't pack it. **You did**.

I unpacked it, expecting to see a whole item and it literally fell apart in my hands. Yet, you deny responsibility. That vase was 125 years old and you broke it. Here is what I think: Your heavy-handed **gorilla-like movers**, threw something on top of the box and broke the vase. Sorry, I take that back, a gorilla could actually do a better, safer job.

Suggestion: Hire a gorilla next time. People will have more sympathy.

97.

TOO MANY COMMERCIALS DURING TV PROGRAMS

CORPORATE GREED

I know you have to pay the outrageous fees charged by actors these days, but come on guys. Enough is enough! Before I sit down to watch my favorite shows, I have been treated to an onslaught of Progressive Commercials with some annoying woman playing her entire family.

I have endured frenetic Fran fourteen times in the past hour and I am done for the day. How many commercials must I endure during an hour long show? I can actually head into the kitchen and make dinner, return, and not miss a word of my show. Doesn't that strike you as odd?

There are more commercials than show, giving me loads of time to get dinner and the laundry done, in between the commercials and Law and Order.

101 Things That PISS Me Off

Suggestions:

If you must overload us with commercials, how about this?

- Hot Hunks

- Cute, warm and fuzzy animals

- More Hot Hunks wearing smiles

- Matthew McConaughey, driving anything

- Something funny that doesn't start or end with Fran

Just remember, what your goals are. You want people to think of your Sponsor in a positive way. You want your viewers to love your commercials **NOT** fast forward through them. With that in mind,
Here are some more suggestions:

- Wildlife is good

- Fran, the Insurance chick is not

- **Hot, topless hunks** are good

101 Things That PISS Me Off

- Screaming kids are not

- Anything about cleaning my bottom is not

- Nor are those bleach commercials with kids that crap on the floor, no good

What genius thought of that one?

- Victoria's Secret is good

- Fat chicks in skimpy lingerie, not so much

- The disheveled Trivago guy not, but when he cleans up, good

I hope that helps your structuring of commercials. Less is more and better, because you don't want me and other viewers just fast forwarding through your money pit.

98.

PARENTS WHO CAN'T CONTROL THEIR CHILDREN

A BASKET FULL OF HOPELESS

I know you think it's super cute when little Johnnie runs around the restaurant, visiting other diners in his cut off shorts and shirt, carrying his **Star Wars laser gun** and screaming with delight. But, trust me, it's not! Your little urchin, standing at my table in a dirty pair of coveralls, is anything but cute. I am trying to have dinner with a friend, can you not see that?

Frankly, I have my own kids, and as you can see, they are **not with me tonight**. I have taken the night off for some **ME** time. But there you are, at a fancy restaurant, one with four $ signs next to it in the menu, but clearly, **NOT** enough money for a baby sitter.

I don't want to hear little Johnnie screaming and yelling while you and your dinner partner sit there mindlessly. You guys seem so immersed in deep conversation. How very sweet! You have all but tuned out little Johnnie. But I can't tune him out. I can't ignore him. He's here, using his **laser gun on my baked potato**, while you and your partner are laughing it up. Lucky you! But here's the deal:

101 Things That PISS Me Off

He's your kid and it's **your** cute! So, excuse yourself, get up off of your ass, round him up, remove him from our presence and take the laser with you. My baked potato is fully cooked thank you.

The Best Pissed Off Ending Ever!

Criminals!

"I Can Change, Really I Can!"
"NOT GUILTY!"

99.

FALSE AND MISLEADING ADVERTISING FOR PRODUCTS

CORPORATE GREED

There they are, those salacious headlines screaming to be read. I'm aware that Oprah is running away with the Postman and that Tom Cruise has learned the Secret of Youth. I have already heard that Cher summited Mt. Everest in a feathered boa and that Brad Pitt is leaving Angelina for the President of Albania. So what else is new? I love a great headline and usually fall for your lies hook, line and sinker.

Once I have clicked or opened up the page for the article, I find it is a misleading ad for some beauty, health or financial product. There ought to be a law against false and misleading headlines,, but there isn't. If there was, you would go directly to jail and not pass go. Frankly you are nothing more than bottom feeders and should be treated as such. Catfish and snails have more integrity than you do. That's not saying much.

How about this for a headline: Publisher jailed for not revealing the Secret of Youth? Or, Publication sued for lying about Oprah running away with the Postman? The only reason you basically lie is to hook people in, like fish, to your website. Then, you continue to harass them using their email or phone. I know better now and I don't click ads where it claims that Gwenyth is cheating, or Cher disappeared, or Oprah ran off and got married. I just laugh and move on. Shame on you!

100.

MOTHERS WHO NURSE OPENLY IN PUBLIC PLACES. DEFINITELY NOT POLITICALLY CORRECT

A BASKET FULL OF HOPELESS

Mothers everywhere take heart. I love you and you are loved by the millions of minions who follow your Earth Mother activities, moment by moment. However, surprise, mothers everywhere, you are not in Africa, nor India, nor even the fields of Thailand.

101 Things That PISS Me Off

When I last looked you are in the USA, in a public place, perhaps, a fancy restaurant. Let's stop with the Mother Earth bit. Yes, in Third World countries, women strap the baby onto their backs or fronts with a piece of fabric. They nurse openly and it's a way of life. They also have babies in the fields and are nursing as they are picking corn, or tomatoes. You are probably not dropping your Mother Lode on Park Avenue, or in a field. I don't see you with that infant strapped to your back or front with anything, but an expensive baby sling. This is no time for the Mother Earth routine. You are at a fancy restaurant, child in tow and patrons such as I, trying to enjoy their overpriced meal.

Step into the ladies room or at the very least cover up with a diaper or chic little scarf from Armani or Gucci. Frankly I don't' want to look across the dining room at Spago or The Bistro and see your boobs hanging out.

After all, I have to believe that you have not been taking your top off at the local Burger King lately, when you don't have your baby with you. **SO** why would you do it now? I get that this is a Political statement, but you can stop now, as you have made your point. I think what you are doing is wonderful and an intimate moment with your baby. **Suggestion**: Just stay home with your baby and enjoy the intimacy of nursing. Just don't make it a public affair please.

101.

PEOPLE WHO GO TO THE THEATER LOOKING LIKE THEY JUST GOT OUT OF BED

A BASKET FULL OF HOPELESS

Don't you have a full length mirror in your home? You have just arrived at the theater looking like something the proverbial cat dragged in! Seriously, what are you thinking? I realize you work all day, or maybe not. Maybe you simply lie around on the couch, watching videos or playing games in your pajamas. But tonight is a special occasion. You have spent actual money on some tickets to see a concert. That is, unless you won the tickets playing Bingo at the local Community Center.

You are a mess! Most of the theater looks like alien nation, because it isn't just you, it's you times 100. If you think the **"SLOB"** look is in style, I have news for you. So how about taking five and freshening up? You could run a comb through that matted mess of hair. You could put on a clean shirt and a pressed pair of pants. Enough with the torn jeans already. Save that look for the local Flea Market.

How about a dash of makeup or some cologne? Make

it appear like you actually care about how you look. But you don't! Frankly, you look like forty miles of bad road on steroids. Did you just get home from a hard day on the farm in your rumpled plaid shirt and jeans? What's with the raggedy sneakers? While we're at it, don't you have a brush?

Your hair looks like you woke up after a night on the town drinking! Have some pride dude. Take care of **YOU**, because if you don't do it, no one else will. **Then you die.**

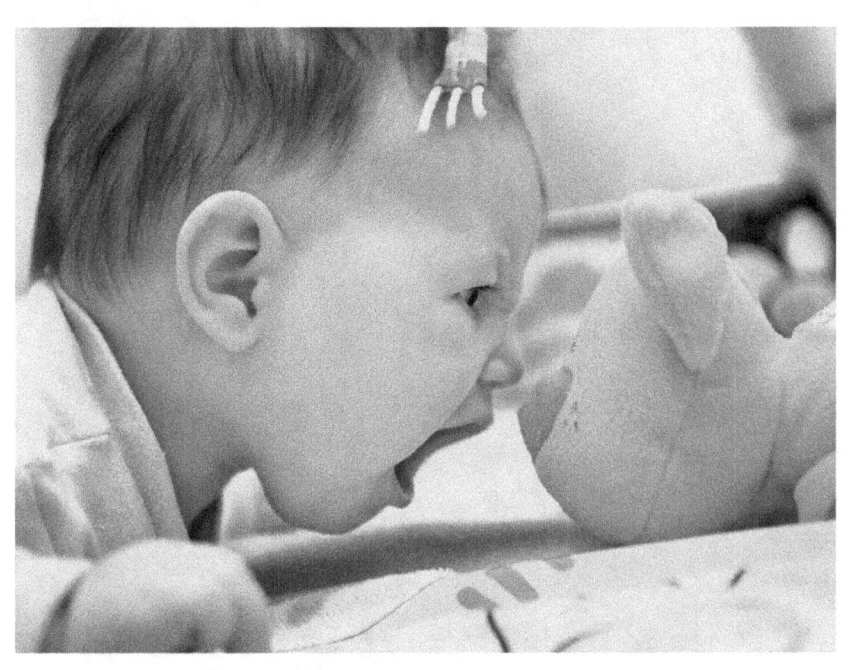

There's A Whole Lot More That Pisses ME Off So Watch For It!

"YOU Really Pissed Me Off Dude! That's Going To Be Number 102!"

101 Things That PISS Me Off

Okay, so you are now mortally wounded and offended by my 101 Things, at least some of which you have probably experienced yourself or even done yourself, at least once. Perhaps you are even one of the guilty people who cross in the middle of the street or turn in front of someone while going 2 miles an hour. I don't know.

What I do know, is that I have only scratched the surface of humanity with 101 Things that Piss Me Off. I know as sure as I am writing this that there are another 101 Things that you are dying to get off your chest.

You don't have to stray very far to find rude and thoughtless people doing **unimaginable** things. Just this morning on a short ride to my local bank there were two that stood out. How about this one: I am in the process of backing out of the parking place at my bank.

A car speeds behind me, whirls around the parking lot and zips down the lane for the ATM drive through. He paid absolutely no attention to the fact that I was already half out of the space and would have hit him. He deserves a special place, but I have no room.

Then, another thoughtless idiot, who I am canonizing in the book of Rudeness. Last night on our way back from an out of state trip, we pulled into a Service

101 Things That PISS Me Off

Center for gas. The pumps were full, but I couldn't help but notice the guy in front of us blocking two pumps. The car in front of him pulled out and we pulled in, however, as we passed his big truck, I saw that he wasn't getting gas at all, he was texting.

So here was this thoughtless person, blocking two gas pumps during a very busy time while he texted. He could have pulled to the side and allowed other people to use the pumps, but no, he was supremely more important. There are no words for this guy but there is a category…**RUDE.**

Now it's your turn. Maybe it's something your mother-in-law does that infuriates you. She isn't alone you know. There are mothers-in-law around the world infuriating relatives every minute of the day. Maybe it's some idiot driver or careless waitress or underpaid delivery guy. I want to help you get your anger out in a productive way.

So there is a new book in the works…101 MORE Things That Piss Me Off, Expletives From Behind The Bathroom Door.

Get your pen and paper ready and start making notes of the things that PISS YOU off each day and then send them in to me. Maybe you will have them included in one of my next books.

MEET THE AUTHOR

California girl Georgene Summers is a born entrepreneur with a wild streak in her that just won't quit. An Adventurer, Author, Talk Show Host, Wild-Life Photographer, Strategic Intervention Change Coach, Marriage & Relationship Coach, Know Your WHY Coach, Inventor, Businesswoman, Fashionista, and sometimes whirling dervish the wildly animated Summers seems to have done it all.

Georgene spent several highly successful decades in the fashion accessories business between Los Angeles and New York City when she finally decided to embark on a variety of new careers in rapid sequence. Several years on Wall Street as a Commodities Associate proved to be rewarding but stressful for the creative Summers. In the early 80's she left Wall Street to build a nightclub in midtown-Manhattan the likes of which had never been seen in the city before.

Summers, always just slightly ahead of her time built a 15,000 square foot club that became the "home away from home" for models, chic "Euro trash" and celebrities galore. The club, called Bolero, prided itself on privacy and chic decadence and hosted many hot and happening parties which celebrated stars like Mary

101 Things That PISS Me Off

Wilson of the Supremes, the wild and wonderful Grace Jones, the original Village People, the late Andy Warhol and Lifestyles guru Robin Leach.

Not one to say no to anything she plunged into her next re-creation with a vengeance and started two businesses, one in telecommunications and the other inventing two fitness related items. She currently holds two patents. Since 1996 she has been traveling to Africa, going on safari alone with only her Masai guide Hagai as company. Content on her own dining out in the middle of the Serengeti by the light of a candle or rising at 5 am to the sound of the baboons in the trees outside her campsite she loves traveling into the bush to photograph all of the animals and has now decided to offer her photographs for sale on her website.

In 2002 Georgene made a decision that would change her life as she knew it. She moved to Africa alone. As part of a self-funded Humanitarian Project Georgene started working with Xhosa tribeswomen teaching them how to make commercially viable beaded cellphone bags. . In 2004 after deciding to return to America she met her soulmate.

Her life would change dramatically as they moved from friends to husband and wife New Years Eve 2004. Her formula for relationship success was proven once again.

Since then the enigmatic Summers has been traveling back and forth from Africa to the states working with him to bring focus to the project that has been near and dear to his heart...Bugz a Humanitarian project. Never one to stay still for long, Georgene took another leap off the cliff and went back to school to study with renowned Motivational Speaker Tony Robbins at Robbins Madanes Institute. She graduated with commendations and is now a Certified Strategic Intervention Coach and Marriage & Relationship Coach on a Mission. Just Ask her and she will tell you how she intends to "Empower and Inspire Women with Hope, Courage, Confidence and the Tools to live all of their dreams and realize their fullest potential for growth and greatness."

Leading Seminars, Boot Camps and Retreats Georgene brings amazing tools for change to any event. Getting Rid Of Limiting Beliefs and Fears, Challenge for Change, Who are You and What Do You Want, Change Your Perceptions and Change your Life are just a few of the topics she covers. You won't want to miss a moment of her inspiration.

An accomplished Author who has penned three incredible books on relationships..."The Dating Dance...Confessions of the Spider and the Fly" and

"No One Moved Your Cheese and her most recent one Blind Spots: The Ultimate Guide To Love In The Dark."

She supports orphaned baby elephants through the amazing Daphne Sheldrick in Nairobi, Kenya and is working with her guide on an educational project to stop female genital mutilation among the Masai by sending the young girls to boarding school.

Georgene recently hosted an edgy wildly popular Talk Show on Voice America the largest Talk Network in the world "On The Edge With Georgene Summers."

If you want to know more about Georgene's empowering programs email her at georgene@aworld4women.com

Love Volume 1 of "50 Shades Of Love" A Collection Of Romances? You won't need to wait long for Volume 2. It has been released April 2016 so watch Amazon Kindle and don't miss this amazing read. It's Love like you want it to be. "50 Shades Of Love, An Afternoon of Romances, Volume 2." available on Amazon Kindle.

"50 Shades of Love, Forever Yours, Volume 3" will be released in May. Also don't miss Georgene's Best Selling Book "Blind Spots: The Ultimate Guide To Love In The Dark" Available soon on Amazon Kindle or in Paperback now. Learn all about Who You Are and How To Change Your Behaviors so that you can have the life you only dream about. Find out the Formula for Dating Online and find that perfect someone. Get Rid Of The Fears that paralyze you and learn Georgene's Secret Way to avoid those "sitting by the phone" blues when the guy you thought was the one doesn't call.

101 Things That PISS Me Off

"101 Things That Piss Me Off, expletives from behind closed doors" is the first is a Series. Get ready for the ride of your life: "101 Things That Piss Me Off, just shut up and listen I'm talking," "101 Things That Piss Me Off, bitching from under the toilet seat," and "101 MORE Things That Piss Me Off, there's no stopping me now," are in the works.

Follow Georgene on Twitter @edgygeorgene and on her You Tube Channel edgygeorgene

BLASTS "Just Shut Up and Listen, I'm Talking" every Tuesday.

SUBSCRIBE AND GET YOUR CRAZY ON!

Pick up your copy today of Blind Spots: The Ultimate Guide to love in the dark and start living your dreams.

"Blind Spots: The Ultimate Guide To Love In The Dark."
To Book Georgene to Speak at your Corporate Event or Function Contact Georgene's Office: info@aworld4women.com
Georgene is available for VIP private Coaching. Go from where you are to where you want to be in months rather than years. For more information email georgene@aworld4women.com and Ask about her VIP Program. You can have Georgene as your Private Coach via Skype, Phone or In Person.

http://www.aworld4women.com   http://www.georgenesummers.com
Office: 860 283 2254   Toll Free: 1866-269-6290

101 Things That PISS Me Off

Just One More Thing

I have recently published a Trilogy of Old Fashioned Love stories entitled 50 Shades Of Love, A Collection of Romances Volume 1; 50 Shades of Love An Afternoon of Romances, Volume 2 and 50 Shades of Love Forever Yours Volume 3. They are short stories and all about sweet and caring Love. Romantic, old fashioned and amazing for every age group. Please go to Amazon Kindle and download them. If you like my books then I would love it if you would give me an honest review. Just go to Amazon Kindle and review my book.
http://www.amazon.com/50-SHADES-LOVE-COLLECTION-ROMANCES-ebook/dp/B01DB29LK8/ref=sr_1_1?ie=UTF8&qid=1458753349&sr=8-1&keywords=50+shades+of+love+a+collection+of+romances

Thank you so much I appreciate you my loyal readers. Don't forget "50 Shades Of Love, Vol. 2, An Afternoon of Romances" has just been released in April on Amazon Kindle. Watch for it! The link below will take you directly to it.
http://www.amazon.com/50-SHADES-LOVE-AFTERNOON-ROMANCES-ebook/dp/B01DMSV5P0/ref=sr_1_2?ie=UTF8&qid=1461261942&sr=8-2&keywords=50+shades+of+love

www.ingramcontent.com/pod-product-compliance
Lightning Source LLC
Chambersburg PA
CBHW050629300426
44112CB00012B/1724